Books by Stewart Harral

SUCCESSFUL LETTERS FOR CHURCHES
PUBLIC RELATIONS FOR CHURCHES
PUBLIC RELATIONS FOR HIGHER EDUCATION
PUBLICITY PROBLEMS (*Editor*)

SUCCESSFUL LETTERS FOR

Stewart Harral

Successful
LETTERS
for CHURCHES

TESTED WAYS OF
BUILDING GOOD WILL BY MAIL

ABINGDON - COKESBURY PRESS

NEW YORK · NASHVILLE

SUCCESSFUL LETTERS FOR CHURCHES

Copyright MCMXLVI by Stone & Pierce

Library of Congress Catalog Card Number: 46-21469

C

SET UP, PRINTED, AND BOUND BY THE
PARTHENON PRESS, AT NASHVILLE,
TENNESSEE, UNITED STATES OF AMERICA

To my Sisters

MARGUERITE
VIRGINIA
AND
MARY

CHURCH LETTERS are almost as old as Christianity itself. Through the centuries countless missionaries, preachers, and other religious leaders have spread the gospel by means of personal messages. But strangely enough, many of today's ministers are overlooking the use of personalized letters to vitalize and strengthen their public relations program. This major medium is producing invaluable results for the relatively few churches that are making the most of its possibilities. It can do equally effective work for others.

With most pastors burdened and working overtime, is it important to think about letters? Alongside the major objectives in a church program, aren't letters just trifling matters? We must not forget that each letter is a representative of our church. Is it a trifle to send out creditable representatives? Is it a trifle that our letters create loyalty, promote stewardship, stimulate interest and attendance, win converts, and in other ways bring men and women into the Kingdom?

Letters, of course, can never substitute for the personal ministry of a pastor. But on many occasions they can augment and strengthen the personal contacts. And certainly the busy pastor by combining the two methods can greatly expand the sphere of his influence.

Letters provide a tested way of reaching countless persons —and making them respond. No hocus-pocus is involved. Rather, results come from using certain effective principles in presenting ideas by means of this swift and friendly vehicle of thought.

7

A letter is a unique form of communication and as such has a power and influence all its own. Not just any kind of letter, to be sure, but one which is planned and written for a specific purpose. Letters can be our best advertisement or our worst—what we say and how we say it will determine which.

Success in letter writing does not come from mere rules and a knowledge of grammar. Rather it lies in the ability to select words—the right words—in such a way that the message accomplishes its purpose and yet is unique because *you* are its creator. As Charles Riker says, "It should be YOU —talking on paper."

Effective church letters are extremely hard to find. Many a church whose program is quite excellent permits its daily mail to go on a dull routine and is blind to the major role that letters play in religious activities. Of all the tasks that church letters perform, the most important is to represent ably and favorably the whole organization. In short, they are good will ambassadors. From a public relations viewpoint, the church's letters are—or should be—a bulwark of church prestige and influence, an important complement to a church's entire promotion efforts. For this reason alone, every pastor will find it time profitably spent periodically to study and to improve all letters mailed by his church.

This book is aimed at one of the weak spots in church administration, an activity that nine churches out of ten need to improve, and can improve immensely. Rightly planned and executed, an active letter program will pay dividends. One pastor declares, "Letters are one of the most worth-while activities of my ministry."

It is impossible to trace the origin of some letters which are published in this book. The same is true of many hints and suggestions for letter improvement—each started with someone and has been passed along until its creator's identity has been lost. Most of the unidentified letters are original; in some instances an idea from a good business letter, for example, has been adapted for use by churches. Quite a number of pastors who supplied specimen letters have now moved on to other churches, but in each case the pastor wrote the letter while serving the church named in the credit line.

Acknowledgment is made to the magazines *Church Management, Printer's Ink, Church Business,* and the *Dartnell Bulletin* as sources of many excellent ideas which have been used in this book. Special thanks are due my colleague William H. Butterfield, nationally recognized authority on letters, who read the entire manuscript and whose counsel and encouragement were of untold value. Also, I wish to thank Ruth Howell, Rose Kirkpatrick, and Margaret Tate for assistance in typing. Finally, I would like to express my deep gratitude to scores of ministers who sent hundreds of letter examples.

Stewart Harral

CONTENTS

Planning Profitable Letters

DO LETTERS really matter? Listen: One day while I was visiting in a home, the elderly grandmother showed me a faded letter kept in her Bible. It was a brief congratulatory note written by her pastor in 1907. He thanked her for the splendid work she had done as teacher of a Sunday school class. Did she appreciate it? Only one who has seen the sparkle in her eyes as she reads and rereads it can realize how much. How wise and understanding her pastor was! He recognized this fact: It is the letter that does not need to be written that usually does the most good. "Unnecessary letters"—they carry the most impact! Your church can get along with little letter writing. But what dividends in good will and co-operation accrue from a human and intelligent letter program!

What is a good church letter? It is a planned letter, a friendly message through which you hope to achieve something definite. You must realize that every written word from you and your church will contribute something to your reputation and that of your church. Your letter writing, like your other duties, will build good will and support for your program. Every letter you write makes an impression. You cannot escape that fact.

It is really the church that writes the letter—not you. Your church has one purpose—to transform lives so that they can become more Christlike. Everything that helps your church to achieve that purpose is good; any factor that works against it is bad. That is why you will plan your letters so they can reach out through space and in a friendly way increase the worth of your ministry.

Every effective letter should have at least five basic objectives. It should (1) get attention, (2) arouse interest, (3) create desire, (4) establish conviction, and (5) get action. These five objectives can be used even in a brief message. At first this task may seem impossible to you. But just keep trying, and soon you will develop the knack of making every letter a good letter.

First, determine the purpose of your letter. If you are hazy on this point you are likely to jot down confused sentences, much-too-long paragraphs, and ill-chosen words. Without a purpose, you will get off the course.

After deciding the purpose, then visualize the action you want taken. Think in terms of the response you desire. Do you want the recipient to attend the Wednesday evening service? Are you asking him to donate books to the church library? Would you like for him to pay his overdue pledge? No blanket appeal could possibly accomplish any two of these objectives. Think in terms of the task of each letter. Each message has a particular job to do, a specific target to hit.

The public to whom you write—whether the unchurched or "pillars" of your church—is composed of individuals. The public is collective, but you are appealing to individuals. The person you are trying to influence is real. True, he's just a tiny fraction of your membership. But he isn't a statistic.

Visualize the reader

Get a picture of your reader in your mind's eye. Ask yourself: "What is his goal in life? How does he differ from other

16

persons? What is his interest in religion? How can I catch and hold his attention? How can the church serve him?" He is interested most of all in himself—his family, his business, his hobbies, his views and prejudices. But that's just human nature. You can't just guess what he is really like. You must know him.

Even in planning appeals and contents of a form letter you must think of the recipients as individuals. Just imagine the group sitting in front of you waiting to hear a two-minute message. How can you interest them from the start? How can your brief message be phrased to get action? What can you say to win their co-operation and support? Get the answers to these questions. Then plan your letter so that it carries the power of "personal salesmanship."

Know your reader. This is the first hurdle toward reader interest. Ideas which seem of great importance to you may not interest your reader. Select ideas from *his* angle. Make him feel, "Here's something I would like to do for the church," *NOT*, "Here's something the church wants me to do."

Think your letter through before you begin to write or dictate. Ask yourself, "What is the best way to reach my objective?" Vague statements, excess words, and rambling sentences create detours on the road to action.

Poor planning sends countless letters to the wastebasket. Too many of them are dashed off without the writer's consideration of desired goals and ways of attaining them. Others fail because no thought is given to making the writing stick together, with one subject, one point of view, and a smoothness from beginning to end. In many instances there is no coherence—a quality obtained by logical order, right construction, and the proper use of connectives.

17

Proper planning means that you ask, "To what extent is this letter likely to accomplish its purpose, obtain the desired response, and build good will?"

Outline your message

It is helpful to make an outline of your message before you start writing it. An outline is good insurance against "beating about the bush," against phrases which detract from the main objective. A rambling letter is the longest distance between two points. It lacks compactness, clarity, and force.

An outline can be simple in form and content—just a few notes jotted down to cover essential facts. With such a guide, you can be certain that you are making a "beeline" toward your goal. Glance at this simple outline:

1. Friendly opening statement
2. Director unobtainable
3. Still plan to hold summer camp
4. Will know definitely soon
5. Thank you for interest

Note the many weaknesses of the following unplanned letter:

Dear Mr. Hicks:

It is my purpose to inform you that your continued support of the Church is needed because of the fact that the world chaos at the present writing demands that all of us put our shoulders to the wheel and push forward.

Since we have not been favored with an answer to our communications of recent date, we wish to advise that your negligence has been disappointing, to say the least, and that we are at a loss to understand why you have not availed yourself of the proffered opportunity to make some sort of pledge.

The writer regrets the necessity of calling your kind attention to the fact that we had counted on you. Please permit me the liberty of pointing out that such a situation, even when due to the fact that other letters have been overlooked or misplaced, injures one's relationship with the Church in due course.

Please be assured that your valued assistance is duly appreciated and that every effort will be made to merit continuance of same.

Yours very truly,

Ugh! Could anything be more dull and insulting than a letter like that? Naturally, it leaves the recipient bristling with irritation. It lacks continuity. It gets off the track. Filled with moth-eaten expressions, this letter would rub any recipient the wrong way. A letter should stop somewhere, but this writer keeps going. There is no emphasis at the end; instead, it just "peters out" with a feeble sentence loaded with bromides. Here's what the writer forgot: The only way you can expect a reader to arrive at the conclusion you desire is to lead him there in a friendly, courteous way.

Hints for developing the message

Glance at some of your recent letters. Do you find that you have wasted several sentences before getting into the heart of your message?

In "thinking through" your forthcoming letter, remember that it isn't how much you say but how you say it. If you're an expert you can write a ten-page letter and keep the reader interested every step of the way. There's a lot of difference between a long letter and a "long-winded" letter.

Write briefly, but say everything you must to tell the story. If the letter is to be an appeal for more support for foreign missions, it is hardly necessary to trace the history of missions, give detailed biographies of outstanding leaders, and go into other minute items. For the most part, you will rely on compact, friendly letters. As one authority phrased it, "The road to better letters is the simple one—the straight and narrow, if you wish." But also bear in mind that brevity, an undoubted asset in letter writing, can be overdone. Say enough to achieve your purpose.

Without the aid of a crystal globe, you must try to anticipate the reader's reactions. In this way you try to make your letter answer any possible questions he may ask. Just as the expert salesman must be prepared to meet all objections in his sales talk, so the letter writer must know what's ahead in the reader's mind. Unless you plan for these questions and reactions in advance, the addressee may figure out his own answers, answers that do not always favor you.

Surprisingly rare is the minister who can write a church letter without "preaching." You know the psychological value of selecting a sermon subject primarily for its interest rather than for its inherent worth. Transfer this device to your letter writing and you need not worry about "preaching" too much.

Whatever the purpose of your letter, remember that simplicity of expression is all important. Often a pastor, without too much consideration, uses words and phrases of his calling—to the complete bewilderment of the reader who is unversed in such terminology. Steer clear of expressions like "Synoptic Gospels," "Pentateuch," "Apocalyptic symbolism," "messianic," "Deuteronomic Code," "Extracanonical Jewish literature" and "pseudepigraphal books." Your reader doesn't have time to consult a Bible commentary every time he receives one of your letters.

Remember that a resultful letter must be tuned an octave higher than a routine, perfunctory letter. If it isn't, the recipient will toss it into the wastebasket. To be sure, many personal letters eventually find their way into the wastebasket, too. Unfortunately, these messages failed to create the proper mental reaction—they failed to click. In other words, they failed to develop a mental attitude of receptivity or action, an attitude that is largely the product of a friendly, forceful, interesting approach.

Some letters, because of the nature of their mission, require more planning than others. Letters answering complaints, for instance, should be carefully planned. This is also true of collection letters, which must have a tone of urgency to bring about the payment of pledges, but must at the same time keep the good will of the recipient. Nevertheless, no matter what type of message is desired, careful writing will always be more than repaid by the resulting clearness and compactness of the letter.

Promise yourself before writing a letter that you will not mail the first draft. Instead, read it for typographical errors, cross out stilted and obsolete expressions, and delete discourteous phrases. See that it has simplicity of expression, omit all excess words, and be certain that the opening has attention value. Make the reader feel that your message is for him alone, and put some spirit into what you write. Above all, see that the closing is convincing and effective. Follow these suggestions and your letter will bring results.

Make the First Contact Count

SUCCESS OF your letter depends on several factors, but none is more important than the opening. You must make the first few words—a few fleeting seconds—really count. The more you can woo the reader with words—words that intrigue, that strike bells of attention and pleasantly say "Wake up" to the reader's mind—the more dramatic your opening. Your opening sentence can make or break your letter, no matter what is said afterward. A letter cannot be dull from start to finish as far as the reader is concerned. If it's dull, he'll finish at the start.

To capitalize on these few seconds you must make your letter "click" from the start. You must say something interesting—dramatic—compelling—something *significant*. To uncover the striking feature in a mass of facts and ideas and then weld that feature into the opening sentence is an art acquired only by unremitting thought, practice, and revision.

Be brief. Say something quickly. But brevity does not mean two words or six words or ten words. It means that your important dynamic statement or question or idea should be expressed as briefly as possible. Just as a headline is at least 40 to 75 per cent of the effectiveness of an advertisement, so the opening of a letter is the important attention getter.

Unless you are an expert, you are likely to start your letters with the second paragraph. Too often, the first paragraph is just a "warming up" period. Humanly enough, because we have not planned our approach, we usually start with some hackneyed opening that requires no great mental effort.

But you must get the attention of the reader in the opening of your message. Either you capture his interest there or he "walks out" on you. That first sentence or paragraph determines the success of the letter. It's the "sink or swim" part of your letter, we are reminded by L. E. Frailey, one of America's best-known letter experts.

Make a strong contact

Examine a stack of letters and you'll find that the weakest spot is usually the beginning. Grandfather may have started a letter by stating "Yours of the 14th instant at hand and in reply I wish to state that—." In his day that was the style, but today's effective letter writer will begin his message by saying something worth while. He knows that the beginning is the place to make his first impression on the reader, and he wants to make that impression favorable.

Novelists, feature writers, newspaper reporters, and others frequently write fifteen or twenty paragraph beginnings before they create one which clicks—one which will interest the reader and lure him into the story. They know the strategic position of the first sentence.

Howard W. Newton, nationally known authority on advertising, once said, "Brother, it's not how you like to write it, it's how Joe Doakes likes to read it that counts." That great truth, applied to letters, means that you take careful aim and then fire at your reader in the first few words. That's the crucial moment.

There are, of course, exceptions. Occasionally a striking

illustration will in itself be more powerful than any opening that could be written. At times an attractive layout will do the trick. But in the great majority of letters, written from day to day, the acid test is whether or not the opening induces the reading of the letter.

Avoid weak beginnings

Since your first few words or sentences constitute your first contact with the reader, you must strike hard. If that contact is weak, your letter starts with a real handicap. But if it is strong, your letter is strengthened. Note the following trite beginnings:

> We wish to call your attention to . . .

> Regarding our telephone conversation, I am mailing a record of . . .

> In reply to your valued favor of August 15, I wish to advise that . . .

> We beg to announce that . . .

> In line with our recent conversation, I have the following facts to send you.

Shades of 1864! Smile at those creaking bromides if you wish, but most of them are typical, not exceptional. Each is a sort of preliminary remark. Instead of creating interest, they kill it. Drop all "whiskered" expressions from your vocabulary. Instead of "sleep-producers" use "daze-crashers" —something that will awaken the reader.

You've noticed the tremendous importance of effective opening statements in a sermon. If your message is well organized, you don't stall for time in your introduction. Instead, you say something which strikes an interesting chord among your listeners. You get off to a fast start. You never waste words. Use the same approach in writing a letter— make your first words count.

Writing openings that are good in a variety of letters is a real chore for any pastor. Occasionally they just come, they just seem to flow out of the situation. Usually they are the result of deliberation, of trying and trying again. Some letter writers insist on writing the opening first. Others do better after the body of the letter is written. If it is good, the copy frequently suggests ways to improve the beginning. The main thing is: Take time, plenty of time, to write the opening.

Never fool the reader

Make the beginning interesting, but don't try to hoodwink your reader. He doesn't like "monkey business." If you start with a ridiculous question just to lure him into the message, don't be surprised if he tosses the letter into the wastebasket. Glance at the following examples:

Can you retire at sixty?
If you can, your last days will be happier if you have given regularly of your means to the Church.

Do you want to get sunburned in church next summer?
Why of course not, you say--but that's what may happen if you neglect to send your contribution to the fund now being collected to buy a new roof.

Just how quiet is a church mouse?
We haven't any idea, but we couldn't keep "quiet" any longer about your overdue pledge.

25

Do you want your Church to die spiritually?

Are you a fugitive from members of the Finance Committee?

Do you want to be one of the saints of our Church?

There is no denying that those openings would irritate any reader. In some cases the writer tried to slip up on the reader. Others ask questions too ridiculous to be read. Instead of "selling" the reader on an idea, any of these openings would leave him bristling with irritation. Many a poor letter that strains the patience of its recipient owes its failure to a writer who has strained himself in writing something "catchy."

You don't believe that examples like those given above are actually written? Just the other day I received a letter with the following opening: "Shall we shoot old preachers? No, of course, we won't, but if more isn't done to support them in their declining years we may be blamed for allowing them to perish." Now that opening is startling enough—it caught my attention—but it is poor psychology.

Anyone can devise a startling statement or use a foolish joke or question. But when you use a story be certain that the point of that story is the point of the letter, be sure that it has a logical tie-in with the remainder of the letter.

POOR: Just the other day we ran across something which we believe will interest you.

BETTER: We've got it! In fact, we're so sure that we have hastened to tell you about it.

POOR: Next Sunday afternoon at four o'clock in the church library we shall have the privilege of hearing a lecture by Dr. John B. Smith, author and writer on recreation.

BETTER: A word to the wise: One of the nation's leading authorities on recreation--and a grand person--Dr. John B. Smith will discuss "Leisure for Living" in the church library at four o'clock next Sunday afternoon.

POOR: Sometime when you aren't too busy, I believe you would find it interesting to sit down and figure out if you had one cent and doubled your money each day for thirty days, how much you would have left.

BETTER: Did it ever occur to you that if you were to start with one cent, and double your money each day for thirty days, you would have more than five million dollars?

POOR: In times like these it is necessary to keep abreast of our church movements. So I thought it wise to remind you that our mailing list for CHURCH TOPICS is about to close.

BETTER: Going! Going! Almost gone! We're speaking of our offer to put you on our free mailing list for CHURCH TOPICS, an attractive, newsy publication that you will enjoy.

POOR: In the rush of closing our church affairs for the year, we noted that your pledge has not been paid. Perhaps we failed to notify you. Undoubtedly, you have just forgotten it.

BETTER: Funny how we forget things, isn't it? I forgot something important: I believe you did, too.

You see, it's all in the way you make the first contact. "Lure" quality is lacking in the poor introductions. In the better examples, the "WE" angle has been subordinated to the "YOU" angle. They "strike home" in the first few phrases. Interest your reader at the first quick look and he'll read more.

Choose the best type of opening

Just what kind of beginning to use depends on the sort of letter that is being written. But whatever the purpose of your message, start with a vital personal interest of the reader. Weigh the facts and various possibilities, then select an opening with attention-getting power. It is not enough to fashion a good beginning—it must be exceptional. This means that its reader interest must be pitched an octave higher than run-of-the-mill starters. However, remember that danger lies in a strained effect. It is impossible to expect every opening to sparkle with the same fourteen-carat brilliance, but a twist in that direction will give the letter an intriguing quality.

A crowded opening, which acts like an anesthetic on the reader, results when you pack too many details into the first paragraph. It is much better to make the sentence sharp and to the point. The more directly you get into the subject in the first sentence, the bigger the favor you are doing the recipient—and yourself.

How long should an opening be? That depends upon you and the purpose of the letter. Make it long enough to accomplish its purpose, and no longer. If it takes more than one sentence, make it two, or three, or four. But do it as simply and forcibly as you can. And keep it interesting!

There is as much variety in introductions as there is in the personalities of writers. Consequently, there is no surefire way to get off to an interesting start. Some openings ask a question. Others tell a story. At times, you can use a startling statement. Sometimes a sparkling epigram will do the trick. On other occasions you give a fact or so which makes the reader sit up and take notice. Highest on the list is the opening which conveys good news to the reader. Whatever type you are considering, write from the reader's point of view. Set him up on a pedestal. Make it his problems you're considering, his rewards for his religious activities, his returns from a program of stewardship.

Use positive openings

To be effective, a letter should never start with a negative idea. If your opening statement suggests something undesirable or unpleasant, it will probably cause the recipient to react against the idea. Note the difference in these openings:

NEGATIVE: You don't want a teaching manual which is antiquated, uninteresting, and loaded down with theological terms.

POSITIVE: You want a teaching manual which is interesting, complete, and filled with suggestions for making each presentation effective.

Beware of an introduction which brings unpleasant news to the recipient. At times, of course, your letter must convey information or news that will bring the reader disappointment. If this must be done, don't "spring" it on him suddenly. Find a positive point of contact and in this way prepare him for unfavorable news. In answering a letter of complaint, for instance, get on common ground with the person by thanking him for his letter or by expressing regret for the inconvenience caused him. Search out some point on which you can agree with him, even though this point be merely an expression of sympathy. An opening of this kind disarms the reader and puts him in a receptive mood.

Words in your letter must perform the double job of making clear the message you want to convey and at the same time putting across to the reader your friendly feeling for him. Use plenty of "smile" words. Gloomy words depress the reader; they kill his enthusiasm and response. At times you'll have to tax your ingenuity to discover a positive introduction, but it can be done.

Let's say, for example, that one of your members has requested use of the young people's assembly room for a meeting, but another group asked for it first. Your first thought is: "I am sorry to inform you that the room you requested for March 2 has been promised to another group." Or you might say: "It is with regret that I find I cannot allow you to use the room March 2." Let's try it this way: "Nothing would please me more than to be able to tell you that you may have use of the room March 2. However, on checking our calendar, I learned that the Sororis Club was given permission to use it that night. But we would be delighted for you to use the church parlor or the Wesley Class room." In the latter, the first sentence gets in step with the reader at the start. And the next sentence tells why his request cannot be granted; the third invites him to use another room. Thus he receives "bad news" and is left in a favorable frame of mind.

Get over on the reader's side of the fence before starting your opening. Spend a lot of time learning his problems— his way of life—before you try to get your ideas into his mind. Then you can write something that will influence him because the whole letter is written around him, instead of around you. Then he'll read on and respond.

CHAPTER 3

Tested Routes to Readership

NOW that you've planned your letter and started by catching the reader's attention, you come to the real task—writing the letter. Everything you've done so far was to lure the reader into the message. You must keep the ball rolling if you want your reader to see the final paragraph.

What is the purpose of your message? You start with that and amass the "selling points" which will make the reader say, "I'll do it." Just how far he proceeds with the message depends entirely on its content.

First of all, a letter must be correct in sentence structure, punctuation, spelling, detail, and mechanical layout. Be certain that every letter which carries your signature is neat, well constructed, and attractive to the eye.

Since first impressions are important, pay particular attention to the layout of your letters. Guard against letters with uneven and tediously long paragraphs, narrow margins, erasures, smudges, and other purely physical defects. All of these faults weaken the letter's effectiveness, no matter how well it is composed.

When the reader unfolds your letter, his first quick visual reaction is an important preliminary to the receptivity of your message. Even a mediocre letter can LOOK good. That's the view of W. V. Cunningham, who listed ways of improving the appearance of letters in an article in *Printer's Ink*. Interest is often increased through the use of capital letters, dashes, and underlined words and phrases. At times, you can divide in numerical fashion the points to be emphasized, and set off these points by indentation on both sides. Adapting an idea from newspapers and magazines, you can make use of headlines, subheads, and captions. Paragraph indentation is especially effective in long letters. Obviously, too much mechanical emphasis, which creates a "circus make-up," gives a letter a choppy and uninviting look. But all these devices, wisely used, will improve the appearance of letters and thus give them more "eye appeal."

Avoid careless construction

Many a correspondent is careless in the construction of his sentences and equally slipshod in checking over his finished letter. Otherwise, how could statements like these appear in church letters?

> Thank you for your letter regarding new furniture for the Primary Department, which reached us by mail today.

> Don't burden your wife by asking her to cook a meal Wednesday night; let us do it.

> We have available two game rooms, newly decorated and completely equipped for young persons with indirect lighting.

In each instance the writer dashed off the sentence with haste and carelessness. Just a little thought and care would have prevented these ridiculous statements.

If you would do a good job, you must write as simply and naturally as you would speak to a person in your study. After all, a letter is merely a written substitute for a conversation. Some letters are dull and colorless because the writer uses stilted or obsolete expressions that he would never think of uttering in everyday talk. Whether you are seeking money for a chimes fund, sending a cheerful note to a member in a hospital, asking a layman to become scoutmaster, or requesting books for the church library, the only way to make your letter effective is to be natural—to be your own genuine, friendly self. Make your letter reflect *you!*

Without mental preparation beforehand, you may write a letter and find yourself rambling into irrelevant details, aimlessly repeating the same idea or phrase or beating about the bush. Of course, deliberate repetition for emphasis is sometimes desirable. But pointless repetition of trivial and insignificant points is a time-wasting and fruitless habit.

Hackneyed phrases completely rob a letter of personality. Instead of saying, "I beg to acknowledge receipt," just say, "Thanks for your letter." When you have the inclination to write, "We are taking this matter under advisement," why not say, "We will think this over"? If you take the stereotyped way you are likely to write, "Regretting the inconvenience caused"; but you can improve the phrase by stating, "I am sorry for this trouble." Eliminate the stock phrases and your letter will be more direct, forceful, and natural.

Always be specific

If you want action, always be specific. Tell exactly what you want, what the reader is to do, how you want him to do it. Is he to call a telephone number, sign a card, contact two other persons, be at church fifteen minutes early next Sunday, or merely read the letter? Don't leave him in the dark about what is expected of him.

Tune in on the reader's point of resistance. On many occasions the recipient starts looking for an excuse to throw the letter away and just forget it. Even though your first contact has been strong, he may look for an excuse NOT to react the way you want him to. Answer his negative slants in your letter.

Imagine, for instance, some of the walls your letter must scale in the addressee's mind. He thinks he already pays too much to the church. He's to busy to think about it. He had rather spend his Sunday evenings at home. He doesn't like to call on strangers. Study these obstacles. Learn how to answer them and your letters will bring results.

Above all, in communicating by mail, you must have the reader's confidence. If you don't have it, you must establish it—not only by facts and figures and testimonials, but through the genuiness of tone that shines between the lines. Psychologically, you can't succeed in your letter program merely by offering people something. More important, you must induce them to believe your proposal. What counts is not what you say, but what the reader accepts. Believability —true sincerity—hits the bull's eye.

Emotional force is vital

More important than the dictionary meanings of your words and sentences is the tone-of-voice of your letter. Each letter has a personality, and it is this factor rather than its grammar that brings about a response in the reader's heart. Ask members of your family, your secretary, or your close friends, to read your letters for spirit and tone. Get their reactions and criticisms. In this way you can get a better idea of the emotional force of a letter as the reader will feel it.

The one good test of a church letter is how well it expresses the thought you wish to convey and at the same time causes the desired reaction in the mind of the person to whom you are writing. You don't want him to think you are a "high-brow." You don't want him to think you know all the answers. You just want him to think that you are truly a friend, so that he will be glad to do what you want him to. If your letter has a warm, sincere, friendly tone, your reader will sense it between the lines rather than in the copy itself.

When giving a sermon, you note the reaction of the faces of your listeners. In a telephone conversation you can change your approach when the circumstances demand. But a letter must carry the whole load of reasoning; once it is mailed, it cannot be changed. Even though your letter is brief, it should tell enough to satisfy the reader or bring about the result in his thinking that you seek. Mix equal parts of completeness and compactness in every letter.

Great letters reach the heart. You may have facts and figures galore, but by themselves they are cold and impersonal. Tie them in with an emotional tug before you use them in a letter. Your reader has a head and a heart. Strive to reach them both in every message. Every successful letter writer is alert to people about him, and he knows how to push the right emotional buttons. He knows what makes them "tick," what makes them respond—he has an educated heart.

Flavor with enthusiasm

Get "steamed up" before you start. If you're in the "dumps," tired, or out of sorts, your mood will creep into your letter. As someone has said, "A letter reflects your mood like a mirror." It is an intangible thing—but very real. Whatever kind of letter you write, be certain that it is flavored with a friendly enthusiasm, because the effectiveness of a letter is often determined by its sparkle and animation.

For example, let's suppose that you are urging more families to attend worship services. You could write the usual "bring your family next Sunday" type. It might result in a slight increase in attendance. On the other hand, you could write one with more life and punch. With enough enthusiasm, it will accomplish its purpose. The two letters that follow illustrate the value of an enthusiastic tone in making a message effective.

Dear Mr. Powell:

In compliance with a suggestion made by members of the Official Board at their meeting October 22, I am requesting that more families attend our worship services from time to time.

We feel altogether confident that more of our members will take this request to heart, especially since our church attendance is not at all what it should be.

We trust that you will consider this request, and that we may have your co-operation.

Yours very truly,

~ ~ ~

Dear Mr. Sewell:

A wise man once said, "Some people believe that a church service is like a convention to which every family sends a delegate."

Amusing as it seems, there's a lot of truth in that statement. But we hope it isn't true in our Church, because the morning and evening worship services are planned for the whole family.

Looking over the congregation from Sunday to Sunday, I find that nothing thrills me quite so much as seeing families seated together--worshiping together.

36

Won't you and your family give your Church first place in your loyalty in the year ahead? Come to church as a family as often as possible and discover how much more meaningful your worship experience will be.

Sincerely yours,

Done in a routine fashion, the first letter lacks enthusiasm. Its tone is so mechanical that any possible reader interest is crushed. The second letter has a "contact that counts." Its enthusiastic tone makes the letter convincing and effective. Moreover, it increases the loyalty of family groups toward the church.

Even in composing a form letter, write it so that the reader feels it is for him alone. Writing from the "you" viewpoint doesn't mean that you should refrain from mentioning yourself, your proposals, your ideas—that would result in letters sounding awkward and unnatural. But, whenever possible, capitalize on the personal-message potentialities of your letter. Avoid the "public announcement" type of letter. Glance at the following examples. Which would strike the more responsive chord with you?

> We urge that all members take steps to prevent missing this highly interesting program. We want everyone to attend, because it's something that no person can afford to miss. Anyone who plans to attend must sign and return the enclosed card.

> Give yourself the opportunity of enjoying this highly interesting program. Come! You'll be glad you did. Sign the enclosed card and mail it today.

With its "come one, come all" tone, the first statement is completely impersonal. But the second example talks to the reader—the invitation has been focused on him.

Tact is important

Almost anything can be stated pleasantly or unpleasantly. Unfortunately, few persons realize that the offensive element in letters is not the information itself, but the manner in which it is conveyed. Often without realizing it, letter writers allow tactless statements to creep into their messages. It isn't so much what you say, as how you say it, that makes the reader mad or glad. Don't let verbal thorns rob your letters of their potentialities.

Which of the following approaches would result in your co-operation?

> You are making a big mistake in insisting that choir rehearsals always be held on Saturday night.

> Since Saturday night is a busy night for everyone, you would undoubtedly have a larger attendance of choir members by holding rehearsals earlier in the week.

Collection letters, especially, may have an abrupt tone. You may excuse such a practice by saying, "Oh, it was unintentional." That does not help, because the harm has been done. Instead of bringing in money on pledges, the tactless letter merely strengthens "payment resistance." For instance, you will avoid phrases like the following:

> Apparently your obligation to your Church is of no concern to you.

> How do you think our Church would meet its obligations if all of our members took four months to pay us?

Your complete neglect of your unpaid pledge has convinced us of your unwillingness to co-operate.

Your failure to answer any of our letters makes us wonder just how much your Church means to you.

Such expressions merely create unnecessary irritation which decreases the co-operation of the recipient. Equally important, they lose good will instead of building it. Do any of your letters have a curt tone? If they do, they are not doing their work with full efficiency. Examine every letter with a critical eye. See that it is courteous and that the reader receives the consideration you would like to receive if you were in his place.

Have you ever checked your letters for overworked words and phrases? Look over some of your recent messages and underscore the words you use frequently. Then compile a list of synonyms of the words you overwork most. If we wish to make words perform for us, we must study them as they perform for expert writers. Word magic does not come from books, lectures, and formulas, but rather from studying, analyzing, and experimenting. Analyze the precise meaning of words, so that you can discriminate between them. Then practice using them in your letters. Do this until each letter has individually personalized sentences, specifically adapted to just one reader.

Unfortunately, the most serious fault of countless church letters is incompleteness. Each letter has a specific task to perform, a job to do. But the message may fail in its objective because the writer has neglected to give an essential fact. And often, the omitted fact is the very factor upon which the response depends. Glance at the following representative example:

Dear Mr. Blank:

The first meeting of the committee on missions will be held in the study Sunday afternoon. I have always felt that our congregation has never had enough confidence in the worth and soundness of missions. Perhaps some of the missionaries we have met did not impress us with the abilities, breadth, and statesmanship adequate for so important a task. As the national income has risen, contributions for the relief of the most elementary needs of distant millions have declined. We shall expect to see you Sunday.

Cordially yours,

John Doe[1]

The pastor who wrote that letter left out several important details, including the time of the meeting. Before accepting the invitation, the recipient needed to know more about the nature and duties of the committee. Instead, the pastor gave some views on the failure of missions. Incidentally, the man made no effort to attend the meeting.

Make each letter complete. If a letter fails to answer all questions asked or implied—if it fails to give all needed information—it will result in delayed action, increased expense, and possibly the loss of good will. Guard against lost motion. Say what you want to say in the fewest possible words consistent with effectiveness. But don't be afraid to use a few extra words if you can thereby make your letter easier to understand. Brevity is highly desirable, if your reader fully understands you. But it is much more important to give him all the information he needs. Is all this too much bother? Not if you want your letter to succeed.

---

[1] Reprinted from Harral, *Public Relations for Churches* (New York and Nashville: Abingdon-Cokesbury Press, 1945), pp. 119-20.

Clarity pays dividends

Clarity is the most valuable of all qualities in good letter craftsmanship. You can acquire this priceless ability by doing one thing regularly: Make it a practice to study the letters you wrote yesterday. Read them again critically. How many sentences contained more than one idea? Is the factual information accurate? Is the language adapted to the vocabulary of the reader? How many big words have you used when simple words would have made your meaning more easily understood? Is each paragraph one complete thought unit? Ask these and other questions in analysis and you will vastly improve the force and effectiveness of your future letters.

Strive to make every letter more than just a form message. Never overlook an opportunity to inject a friendly, understanding tone into a letter. In answering a letter of request, for instance, you can do a little more than is expected and thereby show a genuine desire to be helpful. Let's suppose that a high school senior asks you for material to use in a term theme. You can either write a perfunctory response with a polite "I'm sorry" tone or you can write an "extra help" reply. Compare the impressions made by the two letters that follow:

Dear John:

> I am sorry, but we do not have any books or other printed material on church history, and consequently I cannot give you the information requested in your letter of March 15.

> If there is any other way in which I can serve you, please let me know.

> Very truly yours,

Dear John:

I am quite sure that it will be possible for you to write a worth-while term paper on "A History of the Church."

I would like to comply with your request for material on this vital subject, but it seems that I have misplaced a copy of the book "The Church in History," by Nagler. It is just what you need.

See if you can find a copy at the city library and if not, get in touch with the Rev. John Smith, pastor of the First Presbyterian Church. He has a copy and I'm sure he would be glad for you to use it.

If I can be of further help, please let me know.

Sincerely yours,

Intrigue the reader

Just as a novel must hold the reader's interest, so every letter must keep the recipient's attention throughout the entire presentation. So you won't write a letter just to be friendly. With few exceptions, friendliness alone is not the reason for your writing and the reader is conscious of this. Give him a reason to read your letter—from the first word to the end—and he'll read it and others to follow. Make each message arresting, compelling, convincing.

If your letter is to accomplish its mission, it must move along, it must have a certain flow. You will avoid detours, cutbacks, and the human tendency to jump from one point to another. Define your objective. Decide upon the best presentation. Then tell your story in a way which intrigues the reader.

A letter, being a personal contact, has a personality—let's make it a friendly one. You won't get this out of books on letter writing. It's more than a hard and fast rule—it's an attitude. It's YOU. The essence of friendliness is sincerity. If you really like people, if you are deeply interested in them and in their tragedies and successes, then you'll understand them. Friendly letters are not manufactured from blueprints —they spring from the heart. No matter what kind of letter you are writing—to express appreciation to a loyal member, to advertise the showing of a sound movie, or to urge the choir director to begin work on the Easter music—be certain that it is warm and friendly. And of course the letter can't be if you are not; there's no way of putting into a letter what isn't in you.

Now that we've considered some of the necessary ingredients of successful letters, together with suggestions for lifting them from the ordinary into the extraordinary class, is there one thought, more than any other, that should be driven home? Yes. It's just this: Even though you use many types of letters in the administrative work of your church, see that each one makes a friendly contact. Make every letter an ambassador of good will. Do this, and you'll be amazed at the increased returns in understanding, support, good will, and co-operation.

CHAPTER 4

All's Well That Ends Well

WHEN a letter has arrested a reader's attention, captured his interest, awakened his desire to respond to your idea, and made him believe in the proposal, there is still a real job to be done. That's getting the reader to act, to *do something.*

Next to the opening of the letter, the ending is the position of most emphasis. It's easy to end a letter, of course, but it is quite difficult to write a close which induces action. To be smoothly rounded out, the last lines of a letter must bring the reader over to your side.

To be sure, not all letters make the same use of the climax. In some instances, your letter is not an attempt to "sell" anything, but is merely a warm, friendly note. Even then, a mechanical, stereotyped ending leaves a flat impression. But in most letters the ending should be used to bring the recipient to the proper pitch of enthusiasm, so that he will make the desired response.

Visualize your reader as he comes to the end of your letter. You aren't standing near by to answer his questions and excuses. Mere words on a sheet of paper are carrying the entire load of your proposal. The reader must say "yes" or "no." You can't say, "Before you decide, there's one fact I failed to mention." You have made your speech to the jury—there's no appealing the case. What will the verdict be?

Most writers fizzle out at the end of the letter. Most of

them are uncertain about how, or when, to stop. Somehow they cannot make this pivot point strong enough to get a new pledge, inspire a person to greater loyalty, or win the good will of the reader.

Read a stack of letters and you'll see that many writers use a perfunctory close rather than making the final impression count. For example, glance at the following endings:

> Hoping that you'll consider this matter and that you'll come to church next Sunday, I am,
>
> Yours truly,

> Assuring you that your pledge will be greatly appreciated, I am,
>
> Yours truly,

> Hoping that you will mail the enclosed card or get in touch with me by telephone, I am,
>
> Yours very truly,

Rather than keeping up the momentum of the letter so that the finish will be strong and clear-cut, each of those just fades out with a complimentary close. Revised to modern practice, the foregoing examples might read as follows:

> We'll be expecting to see you at church next Sunday.
>
> Cordially yours,

> Your forthcoming pledge will be greatly appreciated.
>
> Sincerely yours,

> Pick up the phone on your desk NOW and call me at 3465 or mail the enclosed card--and I'll carry on from there.
>
> Cordially yours,

Nothing destroys the effectiveness of a letter quite so much as a participial close. Instead of terminating the discussion in a forceful yet friendly manner, it slows the letter down and actually decreases the power which has gone before.

Strive for action

You'll admit that most of us are procrastinators—we are likely to put off until tomorrow what should be done today. Hence the conclusion of many types of letters should aim to get the prospect to take action while the effect of the letter is strong upon him. For the longer he delays, the weaker the impulse will become.

Perhaps the recipient loses your letter, intending to act later. He may feel that he should respond at once, but he postpones the action. Possibly he reacts favorably to your message, but unless you "sell" him on the idea of replying at once, your efforts may be wasted. You must hurry his "good intentions" into action.

A letter that is trying to convince a person of something, and then doesn't ask for action, is worse than a salesman who forgets to cap his sales talk with the "clincher." Of course, a letter is often weak at a place preceding the close. If stimuli have not been arranged before the reader in such a way as to suggest satisfaction from the proposal, the ending of the letter can hardly do its intended job.

To make your conclusion effective, be certain that the whole thought of the letter is crystallized in definite and clear-cut words. If you are requesting some action, the close of the paragraph should state briefly, very specifically, and yet courteously, just what you want the reader to do. This is illustrated by the following closing from a letter written by a pastor to new members:

> Please feel free to call on me, or any of our staff members, whenever we can help you.

In a letter of information, the closing should summarize the presentation, and possibly interpret it from the reader's standpoint. Whatever the type of letter, it should end on a friendly, personalized note. This shows that the message isn't just another copy of Form K-3 and makes the reader feel that you are aware of him as an individual.

Unless you are careful, your closing words may drug the reader the very instant he should be most alert. They may destroy interest at the very moment when it should be at its peak. Notice the positive tone of the following:

> You've got the facts. Now you'll want to attend the Wednesday night dinner and convince yourself that it's all I've said it to be--and more. Call Miss Sessions at 654 NOW for your reservation. You'll be glad you did!

Why is that a good ending? Because it takes for granted that the reader will attend. Also, it urges quick action in making his reservation. The language is simple and direct. And most important of all, the message has a tone of confidence and positive assurance. It closes with a click.

Avoid too many choices

Authorities on letter writing caution against offering the reader a choice of actions. They are of the belief that alternative offers may confuse the prospect and thus delay his decision. Note the following:

If you will sign the enclosed card indicating when you wish your children to attend summer camp, Miss Helms, our youth director, will get in touch with you; or if you had rather, you may want to send your children to the meeting at the church Tuesday night, May 25. Should you happen to be at the church sometime during the week, why not visit Miss Helms at her office? If she isn't in, come by my study.

Apparently the writer had not planned his letter, so as a result the ending is a mixture of suggestions. The parent receiving the letter hardly knew what to do. One definite urge, or not more than two, would have made an effective ending.

How can you determine the degree of insistence on immediate action? This depends on the nature of the proposal, the type of the recipient, and the judgment of the writer. At times, the immediacy of the situation may demand a speedy response. On other occasions, you may use a quieter form and thus allow the recipient more time to decide. Obviously, for some classes of readers the high-powered "Do It Now" urge is inappropriate.

Three types of close

In letters seeking action, you may use one of three types of close—command, question, or suggestion. Undoubtedly the command gives the strongest urge because it is the most direct. Many letter writers feel, however, that through overuse it has lost some of its appeal, so they rely chiefly on a less insistent invitation to act. Here are examples of the three types of closing:

COMMAND: Call Miss Brandenberg at 653 TODAY and tell her that you will attend.

48

SUGGESTION: Try to be there, and bring along any suggestions or ideas that you might want to
present.

QUESTION: Won't you let us hear from you at once?

Speeding up responses

In special campaigns you may use coupons, cards, ready-
stamped envelopes, and other reply forms with letters. A
card may be enclosed with the letter or it may be affixed at
the bottom of the letterhead. When this is done, never allow the card to cover any of the letter itself. The stamped
envelope is effective in bringing back a reply because it suggests the importance of an answer and the fact that one is
expected. In every instance gear the copy on the reply form
to that of your letter. Whatever type is used, call attention
to it in the ending of your letter.

Some routine letters, of course, do not normally adapt
themselves to an exciting ending. But in the majority of letters, the ending should be the point of emphasis. The reader
is most likely to remember the final sentence or paragraph,
because it is the last thing he reads.

As a simple test, examine some of your recent letters. You
will discover that some of the short ones, chiefly those of
one paragraph or two, suffered a relapse in the conclusion.
Expand them a bit and then add a final punch. If some of
the letters are longer than one page, you have probably repeated yourself—you have missed several good "stopping"
points.

Remember that it is the last sentence that gives the reader
the final impression and sticks with him. It is at this point
that you must capitalize on all the momentum that has gone
before. Many otherwise effective church letters are handi-

capped by weak closings such as "Hoping to hear from you at an early date, we beg to remain." Even more tragic is the writer who uses the same moss-eaten ending for all his messages. Give your last line a personalized touch. Instead of a "rubber-stamp" sentence which should be retired because of old age, give each letter a concise, courteous, and clean-cut ending.

Get an urge in the last sentence. It's just a natural way to wind up a sales presentation. Get the prospect over the "hump" of indecision so that he will respond favorably. It's a poor letter that doesn't follow up its advantages, as far as it can, to the last degree. See that each letter tells your story in a friendly and logical way. Then make certain that the ending is clear and forceful. Jump all hurdles on the road to reader interest, and then give your letter a strong finish.

CHAPTER 5

Getting a "Yes" Response

MUCH of a pastor's success as an administrator lies in his ability to gain the co-operation of others. "The real test of a minister's efficiency," said Roy L. Smith, editor of the *Christian Advocate,* "is not the amount of work he does, but the amount he is able to get his people to do. . . . The most effective clergyman is the minister-manager. To him the members of his congregation are the forces he has at his disposal—the capital he has to invest for the Kingdom."

Every pastor must use all possible ingenuity and tact in keeping a large group interested and at work. Day after day he must request the co-operation and help of others. And obviously enough, every time a layman is put to work the load of the pastor is lightened and the public relations program is extended.

Much of the "unemployment problem" in your church is due to one basic cause: many of your members have never been asked specifically to perform a task. Psychologically, we know the ineffectiveness of announcing, "All who would like to help in the community church survey please meet with me in the study Tuesday night." If you really want a working group, you know the necessity of contacting members personally, by using the telephone or utilizing effective letters. In some instances, it is well to use all three methods. Whether combined with other approaches or used alone, friendly letters do have pulling power.

Use salesmanship

In making a request of another, always remember his interests, his point of view. Plan your letter carefully so the recipient will have reason to read it, to agree with your proposal, and then respond. Make every word lead the reader to the definite action you desire. In no type of letter is salesmanship more essential than in the message designed to create co-operation.

The potential uses of the personal letter in getting the co-operation of church members are as numerous as the needs of a church. Writing a letter of this kind is not an easy task, but when the message is forceful, interesting, and convincing, it will bring results. Here are a few examples of suitable letters.

Dear Mrs. Nash:

Good friends like you, we have found, are always agreeably responsive when reminded of a simple way to help others.

We should like for you to see if you have any old toys which might be repaired. Perhaps you have heard that a group of men and boys of our Church will repair them and they will be given to the Goodfellows for distribution to underprivileged children.

So if you have any toys which might be repaired and used again, please call the church secretary, Miss Gleason, at 2345, and someone will call for them.

You will agree that this is a worth-while program, and we know you will want to help.

Cordially yours,

Dear Mrs. Smethers:

Will you do me a favor--one I shall warmly appreciate?

Our Church should have a large representation at the district banquet for laymen at St. Paul's Methodist Church, Seattle, next Tuesday evening, October 5, at seven o'clock. We should like very much for you to go with us.

Dr. Stephen Overstreet, member of the faculty at S--- University, who has just returned from a two months' stay in Brazil, will be the principal speaker for the evening. I have had the pleasure of hearing him, and I am sure that you will enjoy his address.

Just telephone the secretary, Miss Peterson, at the church (3452) before Friday and let her know that you'll go.

Sincerely yours,

~   ~   ~

Dear Mr. Ross:

What's ahead? No one knows for certain, but this one thing is true: Only by reading and studying the best seller of all times--the Bible--can we save our nation and the world. Never was the command to "search the Scriptures" so vitally necessary.

With your assistance we are going to send twenty-five copies of the Bible to boys in the State Training School. Youth needs clear, straightforward Bible reading now to lead them to saved Christian lives, to help them hasten the Kingdom, and to guide them as future citizens.

We shall look for the enclosed postage-free envelope-- containing your check--by return mail. We know the boys will appreciate it!

Cordially yours,

Seeking advice

Dear Mrs. Farris:

Will you favor us with a little advice?

We have been giving a lot of thought lately to ways in which we could make our Church more friendly to all who attend our services, but especially to strangers.

Our Church has a fine reputation for its hospitality to visitors, but we feel that we could improve. And this is where we seek your advice.

We'd like to hear your comments and suggestions at a special meeting of church leaders in the church library at three o'clock next Sunday afternoon.

We'll greatly appreciate your presence.

Cordially yours,

Seeking personal service

Dear Mr. Watson:

All of us are anxious to do everything possible to make the district Teachers' Conference an outstanding success. As you know, we expect more than two hundred delegates from neighboring churches for the coming meeting.

So that we may make the most of the meeting in our church on Friday, November 13, I should like for you to serve on the reception committee from eight-thirty until noon.

You will render a great service to your Church, and I know the visitors will enjoy meeting you and knowing you better.

Cordially yours,

Naming a toastmaster

Dear Warren:

You did such a magnificent job for us at last year's annual Victory Banquet that we'd like to turn to you again for help.

We want you to serve as toastmaster for the annual District Laymen's Banquet, which will be held at our church Wednesday night, November 15, at 6:30.

Please let me know at once that you will serve. If you think of any way in which I can be of assistance, please call on me. It will be a pleasure to co-operate in any way.

Sincerely yours,

Soliciting special funds

Dear Mr. Adams:

I wonder what you are going to do with this letter--

It's another message from your Church--yes, that's what it is. But it doesn't want to end its days in that wastebasket alongside your desk. It's hoping you'll stop and read it and then say--well, something like this:

"Why, here's another letter from Frank Garner--he's chairman of the chimes fund of my Church.

He's been hoping that I would send in my pledge for the new chimes which my Church needs--I believe I'll surprise him by sending in the card.

Say what you will, but he's persistent and is really interested in the project. He was the one who suggested the idea, and he has followed through. Every week he receives pledge cards from more members."

So I'm hoping that you'll stop to read this letter and that this week or next the return envelope will wend its way back home bringing a card from you.

Hopefully yours,

Chairman Chimes Fund

Invitation to special meeting

Dear Mr. Morton:

If you'd like to

GAIN POISE AND CONFIDENCE

DRAW MORE STRENGTH FROM SPIRITUAL FORCES

DEVELOP A MORE UNIFIED PERSONALITY

RID YOURSELF OF FEAR AND INDECISION

--then you'll want to hear Dr. Bertram Ralls review the new book "On Being a Real Person," by Dr. Harry Emerson Fosdick, in the Young People's Room at seven-thirty Wednesday night, May 14.

Here's an opportunity for you. As a matter of fact, this review will give you many valuable suggestions for living more efficiently. We'll be looking for you!

Cordially yours,

The ideal letter of request makes the reader feel so friendly toward you that he wants to do what you want him to do, just because he likes you. Imagine that the reader is seated across the desk from you, and just talk to him. To get results, your letter must transmit your ideas so easily, so precisely, that the reader absorbs them without conscious effort, agrees with them point by point, and ends by responding to your request. Always ask, "What mental reaction do I want to produce?" The answers will tell you what to say and how to say it. Give thoughtful consideration to the feelings of the reader—first, last, and all the time. Follow these guide posts and your letters will bring action.

Increasing Stewardship by Mail

HENRY FORD is credited with saying that he is sure the church is a divine institution, because any other institution run upon similar business procedures would have gone bankrupt long ago.

Nothing is of greater concern than church finance, to ministers and lay leaders alike. Every pastor is concerned with ways of arousing his members to greater realization of their responsibilities as Christian stewards. At all times he attempts to show how financial support is an investment in souls, a way of bringing Christ and heaven to men, a method of giving that lasts through all eternity.

It is a mistake to think that for the average church there is only a fixed amount available. There are always untapped resources that can be secured if the right appeal is made. "Every budget should have a reasonable amount of challenge in it," M. Russell Boynton once observed. "It should preach a sermon on the theme of Christian opportunity. People will respond if it is at all within their ability to do so."

Many and varied are the methods used by churches in raising their budgets. But whatever method is chosen, it must contribute to the conversion of the church to stewardship. After all, the ultimate goal of financing a church is to Christianize the financial habits of its members.

Even though the minister directs a carefully planned campaign—including a survey, conferences and special meetings with leaders, assignment of workers, proper publicity, and other phases—he often overlooks one vital factor. That is the work which effective letters can perform in stressing the significance of investing money in Christ's cause.

Utilize every channel

First of all, the pastor must prepare his people by persuading them of the worth of stewardship. Every channel of understanding—sermons, news stories, stewardship dramas, leaflets, conferences, announcements in the church bulletin, movies, letters—should be used to stimulate interest. In this way prospective donors will realize the needs and objectives, and possible opposition will be lessened or overcome.

Church funds are raised in three ways: (1) by personal solicitation, (2) by public solicitation, and (3) by direct mail, in which letters are the major vehicle, supplemented in some instances with effective and timely printed or mimeographed enclosures.

Campaigns by mail are of two types. First, there is the single message, known as the complete-campaign letter. It tells the complete story, and is not intended to be used in connection with future follow-up letters. Letters in a follow-up series are sent at predetermined intervals of perhaps three days, a week, or even a month.

Planning is profitable

The chief element of success in a mail-solicitation campaign is the plan. The pastor who merely decides to "send out some letters" is foredoomed to disappointment. Both pastor and members of the finance committee should decide upon information and appeals which are likely to produce the best results.

In all fund-raising procedures it will be found extremely productive to use great care in compiling your prospect list. Contributors fall into two types: active and potential. If time permits, a letter should be designed for each type.

Where several letters are to be used in a follow-up series, it is vital to the success of your campaign that you outline clearly beforehand a definite plan of "attack." This outline should be somewhat flexible, because you may decide to await results from the first mailing before starting the second letter. In some instances you can use testimonials and other reactions as timely material for the second message and also with the third.

You may use a single mailing as a test method and then await its results before making other plans. Whether you decide to use one letter or ten, each should be complete in itself. If more than one letter is used, be certain that follow-up messages have a refreshing and different appeal and at the same time repeat certain points that have been selected as keynotes of the campaign.

Although there are no strict rules telling precisely when a letter series will prove more effective than single complete-campaign letters in church finance, experts have given several important observations. The kind of letter to be used will be determined, in some degree, by the size of the church, its objectives, and whether it is able to carry on repeated mailings to its membership. In most instances follow-ups will be necessary. On some occasions an emergency arises and the time factor limits the mailing to one letter. A long campaign is usually necessary when something new is being introduced or when a sustained effort must be made because of the magnitude of the task. Obviously, specific rules covering all types of financial campaigns cannot be given, because each program is to a certain degree unique in itself.

Great letters have a pull. They produce results. Here is one that went to members of St. Mark's Church, in New Albany. Was it successful? The budget was oversubscribed.

Dear Member:

Running a church is Kingdom business. It must be run in a businesslike manner. The Kingdom Roll Call is the business way of handling the material problems of a church.

WHAT IS THE KINGDOM ROLL CALL? It is a chance for every member to prove his love and interest in his Church. It is a method in which you can invest in a Christian community. It is your investment in the character, morals, and good conduct of your family, neighbors, and friends. It is like the Every Member Canvass that you are familiar with.

WHEN IS IT? It will be held Sunday, November 12. The pledges will be distributed, filled out, and gathered in at the regular church service. They will then be consecrated on the altar. If you are not able to attend the church service, the committee will visit you on that Sunday afternoon in your home. Please try to attend church that day.

WHAT SHALL I PLEDGE? Pledge as God has blessed you. What is your Church worth to you? What is your faith worth to you? Back up your conviction with your pledge. Keep your Church up to the standard of present-day living. Your pledge is not _giving_ to God. It is _paying_ God what you owe him. Pay your debts to God.

AND IN ADDITION . . .

St. Mark's is calling on you to invest in its future. A second, or pink, pledge card will be given to you. On the white pledge card you pay what you owe God for current church expenses.

But on the pink card you will be asked to make a SACRIFICE for the future development of your Church.

The regular pledge is paid during 1945. The special pledge can be paid any time in the next two years. Consider your assets. Count your blessings. Consult your income tax form. Then decide how much you can sacrifice to invest in a greater St. Mark's.

Remember the date, November 12. Plan to attend church that Sunday, and all will be explained in detail.

Your Church Council [1]

An unusual approach

Sometimes it is rather difficult to get away from the stereotyped "you will be asked to pledge" approach. But here's a letter which is different. Because of its unusual approach and completeness it proved most successful.

Dear Friend:

It seemed that I was in the eleven o'clock service February 25, 19--. "Is this Easter?" I asked, for the sanctuary was crowded with folks, young and old, and a line eager to enter reached the street.

"No," said someone. "You should know. This is LOYALTY SUNDAY, and all members and friends were asked to come and show their gratitude for the Church and their desire to continue its work."

What a service that was! Dr. Warren H. Denison spoke of the high privilege of giving, of the fact that there is no place to turn, except to the Church, for the strength which all of us need in these days. Then--at a call--seventy-five men who were to visit in the homes streamed to the front, with a strange, glad expression in their eyes. It was all so enthusiastically and joyfully done.

[1] Used by Theodore Tiemeyer, pastor St. Mark's Church, New Albany, Ind.

That afternoon, when the men went out, they were so happy about it; it seemed to be a game they were playing, not a task at all. When they neared the homes--all families of the parish had been asked to stay at home--they were cheerfully greeted by every member of the household.

Late in the day, when the pledges rolled in, it was found that the budget for Church Maintenance was actually oversubscribed and the World-Sharing (missionary) pledges had reached a new high, the amount expected from a church of this size. Was the minister happy? Yes, and the trustees--they were speechless with delight. Just think! DONE--all in one day!

It turned out that everyone had pledged--given all he could: members of long standing and new standing, members of the congregation looking forward to membership, friends of the Church anxious to have a part in our service to the community and to the world, brand-new comers in the parish, parents of the Church School pupils who wanted to support the Church which makes possible our Church School, friends and members who had moved away but had sent in their pledges.

It was wonderful! I was just saying to Elizabeth, "Am I glad to be pastor of such a church! I'll bet there isn't another like it!" when I awoke. She was calling me: "Carl, hurry, or we'll be late for Loyalty Sunday."

I grabbed my hat. It was a dream--but MAYBE NOT A DREAM.

Will you help make it come true?

You can do it. WILL YOU?

See you in church Sunday.

Your minister,[2]

[2] Carl S. Weist, pastor Community Church at the Circle, Mount Vernon, N. Y. Reprinted from Harral, *Public Relations for Churches* (New York and Nashville: Abingdon-Cokesbury Press, 1945), pp. 125-26.

Letters used in church financial programs need not be dull and lifeless. Nor does the pastor need to write them all. Quite often the chairman of the finance committee writes a letter. Note the following:

Dear Mr. Bleyer:

Someone once said, "If you want the winter to pass quickly, sign a note that's due in the spring." To which I might add, "If you want the months to pass quickly, serve as chairman of the Church Finance Committee."

It just doesn't seem possible for members' names to turn up so quickly with a whole year's pledge past and paid, and the question of another pledge coming up again.

But--the records say this is the case.

Our Church has made remarkable progress during the past twelve months. Under the fine leadership of the Rev. B---, we have had one of the best years in our history. And with your loyal support, we know that another great year is just ahead.

In order to avoid "follow-up," please sign the enclosed card and mail it to Miss Crippen, our secretary. We'll appreciate it.

Cordially yours,

Chairman of Finance Committee

Brief notes are effective

Because they are frequently "sermonettes," stewardship letters are longer than some other types. But not all of them need be long. In some instances you can write, rewrite, boil down, and prune your letter to its essential details. Here are two examples of brief letters.

Dear Mr. Wallace:

FIRST CHRISTIAN CHURCH PAYS OFF DEBT

Wouldn't it give you a thrill to see that headline in the Duncan "Daily Times"? Well, that headline will appear one of these days, because we lack only $875 on our debt.

So what I'm going to ask is--could you help us in ridding our Church of this debt? You have always been more than generous in supporting the Church, and I felt that you would be glad to make a "plus" pledge at this time.

With everyone sharing in this project we shall soon be able to clear our Church of debt. Since we are so near our goal we cannot fail. We shall be expecting your reply soon.

Cordially yours,

~ ~ ~

Dear Friend:

Balance the budget!

That's a most familiar phrase these days. To balance the budget, whether governmental, business, personal, or health, we must have an income equal to the expenditures. Of course, we expect our Church to balance her budget--but this can be accomplished only through the contributions of her members.

Our Church's income is dependent upon the stewardship of her members, and our stewardship is in ratio to our love of God and loyalty to his Church.

We're expecting you to attend church next Sunday, November 15, and to make a pledge. Remember that "Giving is a vital expression of one's religion."

Cordially yours,

Finance Committee [3]

[3] Used by First Presbyterian Church, Springfield Gardens, N. Y.

Pre-campaign announcements

At times, it is desirable to use an introductory letter which announces a coming campaign, for in this way members will be prepared to make a decision later. Here are two letters, the first from the chairman of the board of stewards and the second from the finance committee:

Dear Church Friend:

As our church year draws to a close, your Official Board, to whom you have entrusted the privilege of representing you in Methodism, is happy to give an account of its stewardship in this message of the "state of the Church."

Your Official Board wishes to express its appreciation of the splendid work of our pastor, the Rev. James R. Uhlinger, and to express his and our appreciation of your faithful co-operation. This has made possible a grand forward movement all along "the home front."

We feel that we have every reason to be proud of the type of Christian effort that is being exemplified in every department of our church activities, and we firmly believe that this has been made possible only by the love and loyalty of OUR UNITED CHURCH.

NEXT WEEK you will receive a message from the Finance Committee giving in complete detail the entire financial need for the coming fiscal year, which begins May 1. You will learn of our plans for CONSECRATION OF PLEDGES on Easter and for completion of the EVERY MEMBER CANVASS for expenses and for world service.

Think it over--be much in prayer--be ready to assume your full share of financial responsibility in the same fine spirit which has made it possible for us to pay all our bills promptly without a deficit and with a comfortable sum in the treasury to take care of emergencies. With your loyal co-operation all will be well again.

Faithfully yours,

C. Ross Smith
Chairman of the Board [4]

~ ~ ~

Dear Methodist:

We are now within ten days of the close of our church year. May 1 opens the new year.

The NEW SUGGESTION SHEET is enclosed for your use in determining what your fair share shall be if the budget is to be met in full. Please read the introductory statements at the top of the sheet carefully before you study the budget and look for your name.

REMEMBER--if you join all the others in accepting the suggestion listed with your name, our Church will completely cover its operating expenses and all incidental items, and our program of service for 19-- can be enlarged rather than curtailed.

A church pledge is not just another contribution to one of the "causes" which annually appeal to you. A CHURCH PLEDGE IS OUR WAY OF SHARING WITH GOD IN FULL RECOGNITION OF THE FACT THAT ALL WE HAVE COMES FROM HIM.

Your pledge card is enclosed for you to fill in after due thought and prayers.

BRING YOUR PLEDGE CARD WITH YOU WHEN YOU COME TO CHURCH ON EASTER SUNDAY--this coming Sunday, April 25.

[4] Used by First Methodist Church, Shenandoah, Iowa.

In a simple and very impressive service at the close of the great Easter church service all of us as we leave the sanctuary will place our pledges upon the altar in the presence of the Living, Risen Christ.

Those who are out of town on Easter will be given an opportunity to present their pledges at the close of the church service on Sunday, May 2.

"Give all you can" was not only John Wesley's oft-repeated precept but the pattern of his life, and it is that spirit which has built the local Church of which you are so proud. Let this be our motto:

THE MORE I GIVE

THE MORE I LIVE

Sincerely,

The Finance Committee [5]

Quite a number of church members who dislike being solicited by an official must sometimes be reminded a second time that their pledges should be sent in. Here is a letter of that kind written by Ernest Fremont Tittle, pastor of the First Methodist Church, Evanston, Illinois:

Dear Mr. Crossett:

We have extended the period of unsolicited giving to the Church. There are now churches in this country--a splendid few --whose budgets each year are raised without personal solicitation; we want First Church to be one of them.

We all recognize that personal solicitation should not be necessary, especially in such a time as this. So I am assuming that

[5] *Ibid.*

68

you will be glad to sign the pledge card enclosed for as large an amount as provided in this mailing. I will then see that your name is withdrawn from the list of those who will be personally solicited. The "house-to-house" canvass will start Monday night, October 23.

It is now quite clear that without more of the things Jesus Christ stands for the world is destined to appalling suffering and destruction. We must, therefore, uphold the Church by "our presence, our prayers, our gifts, and our service."

Sincerely and gratefully,

Ernest F. Tittle

Boosting present pledges

On some occasions when you desire increased pledges from those who consistently support the financial program of the church, a special letter may be used. Here is an example of an effective message:

Dear Friend:

With business letters, the briefer the better. With love letters, the longer the lovelier. This is both, but mostly the latter-- as you'll see.

Because you are a supporter of Central Methodist Church we know you must love her, otherwise you'd doubtless get a divorce. But there are such different degrees of affection--all the way from cold deference to passionate devotion.

Do you agree that, other things being equal, the intensity of our love is pretty fairly revealed by our eagerness to give her the utmost possible--in money, as well as in time and service.

Perhaps you really love your Church more than your subscription shows and you are glad of this chance to increase your contribution now. Perhaps you could double, or even treble, your present gift. That would be very wonderful!

The fact is, we, the present membership of the Church, are actually not paying our way. Much of our current expenses are paid from our endowment funds. This would not be too unwise were we in normal times, perhaps. But with the present boom--and the inevitable aftermath--do you not agree with the Official Board that we must do our utmost to avoid drawing from our "sinking fund" now, lest it be exhausted when subsequently we shall need it desperately?

Surely you won't consider this letter a "dun," nor even a call to duty. It's merely an affectionate suggestion that you indulge in a real delight--showing your loyalty by your devoted support. Your Church is no club to which you pay dues. It is a Cause to which you commit your utmost.

Will you consider this whole matter conscientiously now, in communion with your God, and if you have not already done so, make the whole transaction a true sacrament?

We eagerly await your response.

Most loyally yours,

Henry H. Crane [6]

Alert pastors have discovered that church members temporarily living in other cities should be given opportunity to pledge. Since there cannot be any personal solicitation in such cases, letters provide the only practical means of making the contact. Note the following example:

[6] Pastor Central Methodist Church, Detroit, Mich.

Dear First Church Member:

Since you received a copy of our year-end report, early in October, you have heard nothing further from us with regard to the campaign to raise the current-expense budget for 19--. While you are away from Evanston we just don't expect you to give us the same degree of support you did when you were here.

This year we set out to raise the entire amount needed in pledges ($81,000) during the fall campaign, which ends with the Ninetieth Anniversary Dinner, November 21.

As of last Sunday, we had pledges for $75,920.06! This is by far the largest amount received by this date since "the good ole days" of 1929 when First Church was heavily supported by a few wealthy and generous members.

For many years after his retirement, one of these generous supporters continued to send us an annual check for $2,000. Last year we recognized the fact that he had done his share as a non-resident and did not ask for a renewal of his pledge.

But we are willing to accept smaller subscriptions; and enough of them would compensate for the loss of this $2,000 and go a long way toward supplying what we need to attain our goal.

It might interest you to know that many of our local members have this year made larger subscriptions than ever before. When we last checked it, increases had been made by nearly 40 per cent of our people. These increases account, of course, for the showing we have made to date--which is $10,000 ahead of this date last year!

It is the fact that you have kept your membership here in spite of your absence that makes us feel free to tell you our story. Your interest in First Church is one of our real assets.

Because we feel that you may want to have some part in

our program, we are enclosing a pledge card and an envelope that requires no stamp.

Very sincerely,

Harlan G. Greenfield
Chairman, Finance Committee

P.S. If you should be in Evanston, we hope you will pay us a visit. This fall Dr. Tittle has been preaching some of the greatest sermons of his career.[7]

~ ~ ~

Dear Member:

DO YOU WANT TO LIVE? We all do. Jesus teaches that a person lives in proportion as he invests himself in other lives. There is no promise of living forever made to the man who spends himself on himself. A man is as immortal as he is useful. He lives as long as the thing in which he has invested lives. "Every institution is the lengthened shadow of some man."

DO YOU EXPECT TO DIE? We all do. We all must. The moving picture said, "You can't take it with you," meaning money. Yes, you can. Money, like life, may be mortal or immortal, depending on the use which is made of it. Your money can go with you where nobody can squander it. How? No, you don't gather it up and put it in the shroud you expect to wear. What a man takes with him from this earth depends upon the way he has invested his life and his money. His investment can be immortal.

HOW TO INVEST. The man who invested his money in the education of Wilfred Grenfell, Booker T. Washington, S. Parkes Cadman, Albert Schweitzer, or T. Kagawa will have that

[7] Used by First Methodist Church, Evanston, Ill. Ernest Fremont Tittle, pastor.

investment with him through all eternity. You can think of some others who went out from this Church in whom our people invested. Money, when put on the altar of your Church, purchases a policy in terms of life--for you and many others. You pay the premium; the Lord produces the benefits to the world in the coin of LIFE. That life is immortal. Therefore you are not leaving your money behind. It is your life, your very soul.

THE TEST OF LOYALTY. The acid test of Christian earnestness lies in the use of our money. Money talks very loud. Unless our money is on the altar it is not likely that our heart is there. This is central in the teaching of our Master. One out of every six verses in Matthew, Mark, and Luke deals with the use of our possessions. In the teachings of Jesus you and I are not owners but rather stewards of what we have. Does the use of our money square with our profession of faith?

THE CONCLUSION OF THE MATTER. A man is worth just about as much as the things he is living for. He will give to the things in which he is interested and in which he sincerely believes. Do you believe in the investment your Church is making in lives in this community? Your support will be your answer.

Faithfully yours,

Stanley Sellick
Pastor [8]

Special campaign letters

Most churches must conduct several financial campaigns each year for special projects and enterprises. In many instances little, if any, personal solicitation is done; instead, pastors make use of letters. Here are a few examples of letters which performed their functions successfully.

[8] First Congregational Church, Stratford, Conn.

Dear Member:

Again we come to Palm Sunday, Holy Week, and Easter anniversaries, when we expect to rally our membership from near and far. May the Season bring you its peculiar blessings and inspiration. We offer you our program in outline and covet your presence and co-operation in making the most of these high days in our Church Year.

Palm Sunday means a joyous day for the christening of many of our Cradle Roll babies, for receiving into our membership by confession or transfer our largest group of the year, for special music and the sermon. My subject this year: "The Timely and Timeless in Christ's Triumph." If you know of any prospects for our Church, will you please send in their names and addresses, or phone them to the office at once?

We plan to participate with our neighborhood churches in Holy Week services from 12:20 to 12:50 P.M. at the First Presbyterian Church, Van Ness Avenue at Sacramento. The following ministers will speak in the order named: John C. Leffler, Henry C. Warber, Edgar A. Lowther, Jackson Burns. On Good Friday, April 7, we will conduct our Three Hour Service from 12:00 until 3:00 P.M. in our main auditorium. "The Seven Last Words of Christ" will be interpreted by the choir and guest ministers.

Our Easter Sunday sermon, on the theme "Alive Forevermore," will be delivered at the eleven o'clock worship. An augmented choir will sing "Unfold, Ye Portals" (Gounod), and other special numbers, under the direction of our minister of music, William E. Knuth. A program for the entire Church School will be held in the Red Room at 10:00 A.M.

We are enclosing herewith an Easter envelope for your special offering, set aside this year for the pension fund of our retired ministers. The balance due on our share in the California Conference total asking is $578. A tithe of our income for Holy Week, or one day's wage, will enable us to reach our goal. Will you please see that your regular church pledge is paid up to April 1, so your name will appear on our regular Quarterly Honor Roll of paid-up subscribers? This list will be published in our bulletin for April 16.

Wishing you and yours a blessed Easter, I am,

Faithfully yours,

Edgar A. Lowther [9]

~ ~ ~

Dear Friend:

At the Christmas Season each year it is the custom of our congregation to give some material expression to its gratitude to God for the gift of his Son, Jesus Christ.

It has been the privilege of our Church for a number of years, through these Christmas gifts, to support its own representative in South America. We are earnestly sure that members of the congregation will give as liberally as they can to this worthy cause.

Please use the enclosed envelope or pledge card for your gift, mailing it to the church.

Faithfully yours,

Stuart Nye Hutchison [10]

~ ~ ~

Dear Friend:

It has long been the custom in our Church to give you an opportunity to make a special offering at Christmas. In the

[9] Pastor Temple Methodist Church, San Francisco, Calif.
[10] Pastor East Liberty Presbyterian Church, Pittsburgh, Pa.

season of giving gifts in the spirit of Christ, is it not most appropriate to give a special gift to the Church of Christ, without which we would not know about him?

It is especially appropriate to do so this year in our Church for two reasons. First, the Church is more needed and is serving a wider and a deeper need than perhaps ever before. Second, we are approximately two thousand dollars short of raising our 19-- budget. Your gift will help much to wipe out that amount, which otherwise would have to be carried over as a deficit into the 19-- budget. Let us pay our way year by year.

You will find envelopes enclosed for your convenience. Leave them on the offering plate at either the eleven o'clock Christmas Worship Service or the five o'clock Christmas Candlelight Service on Sunday, December 20. If you find it impossible to attend either service, please mail your special offering to the church office.

Let us celebrate Christmas this year with a new understanding of its spiritual meaning. It is the symbol of God's pledge that light is stronger than darkness, that goodness is more powerful than evil, that the eternal forces of the universe are on the side of the constructive efforts of mankind.

May the richest blessings of this holy Season be yours!

Faithfully,

Harry B. Taylor, Moderator

Frederick H. Biederstedt, Clerk
For the Session [11]

[11] Used by Harry Bertrand Taylor, minister First Presbyterian Church, Syracuse, N. Y.

Dear Mr. and Mrs. Edwards:

In appreciation of all previous responses we again make the request for a special Easter offering. This has been the custom of Johnson Memorial Church for many years.

This year we shall apply the offering to church improvements. We have a wonderful edifice and we must not let it deteriorate.

We are painting church property--both parsonage and the interior of our Sunday School rooms. The Church Board has agreed to share (with the women) one half the expense of correcting the acoustics in our large social hall.

The situation is--these and other improvements call for more than $1200 not in our regular budget. We think that the Easter offering will cover this amount in full.

Enclosed is an Easter envelope for your special thank offering.

If you can afford to help, please bring your offering on Easter Sunday, April 9, or on Palm Sunday, April 2. We earnestly thank you.

Sincerely yours,

L. E. Woods
Chairman of Finance Committee

E. B. Pryor
Chairman of Board of Stewards [12]

Whenever you write a stewardship letter, whether for the regular budget or for a special cause, be sure to give the

[12] Used by Rolla S. Kenaston, pastor Johnson Memorial Methodist Church, Huntington, W. Va.

reader all the facts he will need in order to take the action you are trying to stimulate. Always tie in your cause with the interest of the readers. Use straightforward and forceful language, and be certain that your message is friendly and enthusiastic in tone. End your letter on a constructive note, compactly presented. Write enough letters like that, and you will Christianize the financial promotion of the cause of the Kingdom.

Resultful Collection Letters

CHURCHES lose thousands of dollars each year because many members fail to pay their pledges. Too often a pastor just waits and hopes that somehow the money will come in. Some of it does, of course, but he could obtain a much larger proportion through the use of effective collection letters.

Certainly there is a great deal more to the art of collecting accounts by mail than merely bringing in pledges that are overdue. Even though your letters do show tangible results, you must be certain that your messages have not only kept the good will of members but have actually strengthened their loyalty to the church.

In planning a collection letter, first imagine yourself in the position of the person who will receive the letter. What kind of appeal would make you co-operate? You wouldn't like to be insulted; neither would you like a "pay up or else" hint, no matter how subtle it might be.

Every collection letter has some intangible quality which can either make or lose friends for your church. Above all, let us remember that no normal human being likes to be told that he has failed, that his continued neglect has been deliberate, or that he has ignored past requests.

Why some letters fail

Often collection letters fail because of (1) a curt tone, (2) lack of originality in approach, (3) too much "preaching," (4) a pessimistic tone, (5) poor word choice which makes the recipient indignant, or (6) excessive length. It's the lively, spirited letter that gets attention and results.

In most instances your letter will call the reader's attention in the least objectionable way to the fact that his pledge is overdue. This must be so written that the letter cannot be construed as a dun but will be considered merely a little "jog."

Although the pastor will write and sign some of the letters, it is usually better for collection letters to come from the chairman of the finance committee. Most of the time the two officials collaborate in writing the message, with the chairman sending it out over his signature.

Let's be human

Above all, see that each collection letter is personalized. This means, in the first place, that you should greet the person by name. "Dear Miss Smith" is better than "Dear Madam." If you use all-purpose labels, such as "Dear Member," "Dear Friend," and "Dear Sir," you have missed an opportunity to create a favorable first impression. Even if you are forced to use a mimeographed form letter (which is never as resultful as a typed message), credit the recipient with an individual personality in the salutation.

There is no absolute formula for success in collection letters. Perhaps the letter that Mr. Brown likes would not appeal to Mr. Jones. In every case, know and write to the person as an individual. Sometimes a touch of humor is desirable, but use the humorous letter with discrimination. On the other hand, always give your letter a warmth of tone, a certain vitality, a human quality. Often a church letter is so cold that it sounds like a message from a processor of frozen vinegar!

These brought results

Here are a number of letters that stimulated action on overdue pledges:

Dear Mr. Lucas:

It's a long time from September till July!

Many things have happened since last September. But nothing at all has happened regarding our monthly statements reminding you of your pledge.

Maybe you intend to pay the year's pledge in one sum --maybe you overlooked the monthly reminders-- maybe we shouldn't be sending you this letter--

But anyway, let us hear from you.

Cordially yours,

Chairman Finance Committee

~ ~ ~

Dear Mr. Peterson:

You've heard of the colored minister who preached that salvation is free, and upon concluding, asked that a collection be taken. At this point one of the brethren in the congregation got to his feet and protested, "Parson, I thought you said salvation was free--free as the water we drink."

"Salvation is free, Brother," replied the minister. "It's free as the water is free, but when we pipes it to you, you have to pay for the piping."

81

We all know that salvation is free, but that our church budget is necessary to keep our fine program going. This letter is just a friendly reminder of your unpaid pledge of $8.50. Send us your check today! We'll appreciate it.

Sincerely yours,

Chairman Finance Committee

~ ~ ~

Dear Mr. Sims:

Did you know a church could whistle? Well, we didn't either until one of our fellow ministers told of dining in the home of one of his members.

"Can a church whistle?" the little boy asked the minister. "Why do you ask?" replied the pastor, and the boy said, "Because Pa owes twelve dollars to the Church and he says he's going to let the Church whistle for it."

Well, all of us will soon be whistling, because we lack but $300 on our budget. This letter is just a friendly reminder of your unpaid pledge of $6. Send us your check today! We'll appreciate it.

Cordially yours,

Chairman Finance Committee

~ ~ ~

Dear Mr. Beach:

When one of our members lets a pledge run a trifle beyond the due date, we send a little reminder like this--and nearly always back comes a check in the very next mail.

82

No doubt you have merely overlooked sending us your check for $12 in payment of your November and December pledges, and we are sure we may depend upon your attention to it soon. Thank you.

Cordially yours,

Chairman Finance Committee

~ ~ ~

Dear Mr. May:

Church finance is a peculiar thing. Unlike any other enterprise in the world, our Church, without using curt "Collection" letters, raises its entire budget through the loyalty and co-operation of people like you.

So this letter is just a friendly reminder of your unpaid pledge of $12. We shall look for the enclosed postage-free envelope--containing your check --by return mail. We'll appreciate it!

Cordially yours,

Chairman Finance Committee

~ ~ ~

Dear Mrs. Swenson:

I know your pledge is "as good as gold."

I also know that this amount is small and--in the press of other matters--has probably been overlooked.

Most of our budget is made up of small pledges, and when they are not paid promptly our whole financial program suffers.

We feel certain--now that this obligation has been brought to your attention--that you will take care of it immediately. This favor will take only a minute of your time, and it will help us very much. Thank you.

Sincerely yours,

Chairman Finance Committee

~ ~ ~

Dear Mr. Ransom:

Don't apologize.

I send out dozens of reminders each month. Yes, and I receive them, too.

I haven't the slightest worry concerning either your willingness or your ability to send us a check for $4.50 for your December pledge.

Send it today! We will surely appreciate it!

Cordially yours,

Chairman Finance Committee

Dear Mr. Reynolds:

HOW ABOUT--

a little pen

a little ink

a little time

a little think

a little check

short and snappy

is all we need to make us happy

--referring, of course, to the $24 due on your pledge.

Sincerely yours,

Chairman Finance Committee

~ ~ ~

Dear Mr. Washburn:

A collection letter is a good deal like a proposal of marriage. You can beat around the bush and take up a whole evening with the girl of your choice, when actually all you want to say is, "Will you marry me?"

Collection letters are like that. We hunt around for trick phrases and try to think up new avenues of approach when really all we want to say is, "Will you send us a check?"

Amount due: $30

Cordially yours,

Chairman Finance Committee

Dear Mr. Landsaw:

I wish it were possible for me to call personally for the amount listed above.

Since I cannot have that pleasure, I am doing the next best thing. I am sending a messenger. He is attached to this letter. This messenger of mine will make the round trip, no charge to you, in good time, provided he is not held up at your end.

Will you please enclose your check and get him started back on the way today?

Sincerely yours,

Church Treasurer

[Postpaid envelope is enclosed with this type of letter.]

~ ~ ~

Dear Mr. Browne:

When a Mexican says manana, he literally means "in the morning," but without giving it conscious thought he intends to procrastinate to some dim future time.

Perhaps we have been saying manana too long in writing you about your overdue pledge--and perhaps you have, with all good intentions, been mentally saying the same thing.

Doubtless you have just overlooked your pledge of $15. We shall appreciate receiving your check within the next few days. Thank you!

Sincerely yours,

Chairman Finance Committee

"Thank you" builds good will

The church member who attends to his obligations promptly is entitled to an occasional word of recognition and compliment. Too often such a person is forgotten in the stampede of reminders directed to those who are not consistent in meeting obligations. It takes only a few minutes to let a faithful member know that you appreciate his loyalty and co-operation, and such thoughtfulness is sure to build good will for your church. Never allow a prompt-paying member to become the "forgotten man" in your financial program. Write more "thank you" notes to persons in recognition of their dependability as stewards.

Forward-looking pastors are finding that letters to those who are punctual in meeting their obligations are worth many times the cost involved. The letters that follow illustrate ways of recognizing and complimenting church members for their excellent support:

Dear Mr. Hughes:

This note is written to convey our sincere thanks to you for the prompt manner in which your monthly pledges are always paid.

It has never been necessary to remind you of a past-due pledge. While this may not mean a great deal to you, to us it marks you as one of our most loyal and devoted members.

Thank you again for your fine record of promptness.

Cordially yours,

Chairman Finance Committee

Dear Mrs. Bendeum:

Yes, this is a letter from the chairman of the finance committee, but it is far different from one you might expect from me.

Its purpose is to express our thanks for the pledge which you have made to our Church for the coming year. Because of many new challenges and problems, our Church must be kept strong in the critical year that lies ahead. Your generous support is appreciated now more than ever before.

So thank you again for your part in helping our Church to meet its responsibilities in the year ahead.

Cordially yours,

Chairman Finance Committee

~ ~ ~

Dear Mr. Gibb:

If you have ever felt that your long record of stewardship to the First Christian Church has proved futile, that it is unnoticed and unappreciated, you are mistaken.

For fifteen years your prompt payments on your annual pledge have been an endless source of gratification, and they have helped in advancing the Kingdom.

This letter is to tell you that we do appreciate your loyalty and to say: "Thank you."

Sincerely yours,

Chairman Finance Committee

Dear Mrs. Engel:

This is not a request for money, but a letter of appreciation for your generosity.

The generosity of you and others who this year increased the amount of your giving to the Church and thus made it possible for the executive section of the Finance Committee to go on record at their December meeting that, for the second consecutive year, there will be <u>no</u> <u>plus</u> <u>campaign.</u>

Only once before in recent years have we wound up a budget campaign any closer to our goal. But that year the goal was $12,000 less than it is this year.

At the end of the campaign that year we needed only $1,200 to make the goal. This year we were $3,200 short at the wind-up, November 21; but that figure has since been reduced to $2,144, an amount that will readily be forthcoming during the course of the year.

This record was made possible only because you and some 365 others made an increase in the amount you contribute to our budget. Without these increases we would still be $9,268 shy of our goal.

Dr. Tittle and I want to add to our previous letter of thanks a special word of appreciation to you; because, without your generosity, First Church would be in an entirely different financial position today. Increases such as yours this year not only raise the level of giving, but influence every contributor to think in more generous terms.

Best of all, perhaps, is that you will find your greater contribution a lasting source of satisfaction to you.

Very sincerely,

Harlan G. Greenfield
Chairman Finance Committee

To all that is said above I heartily and most gratefully subscribe.

Ernest F. Tittle
Pastor [1]

~ ~ ~

Dear Mr. Carpenter:

This is exclusively a letter of thanks.

Churches, unlike other institutions, depend entirely on the co-operation and fine Christian spirit of people like you. So we want to tell you right now how much we appreciate the consistent promptness with which you have always taken care of your pledge.

Your loyal support has been most encouraging to us and you may be sure that with your help our Church will continue its high purpose of elevating the spiritual life of hundreds in our community.

Sincere appreciation and cordial good wishes to you.

Gratefully yours,

Pastor

~ ~ ~

Dear Mrs. Ray:

Did you ever have the feeling that you were overlooking something important, but yet could not think what it was? So have I. But today I thought of it.

[1] First Methodist Church, Evanston, Ill.

And this is it: A pastor, who is responsible for the entire church program, spends a lot of his time encouraging people to pay their pledges. Often he overlooks people like you who always pay their pledges like clockwork.

You have maintained a high standard in your stewardship toward the Church, and we deeply appreciate it.

Cordially yours,

Pastor

~ ~ ~

Dear Mrs. Sellar:

We appreciate the courtesy shown by paying your pledge so promptly, and we, not to be outdone, return it by saying "Thank you."

Cordially yours,

Chairman Finance Committee

Finally, we must remember that a good collection letter is a sales letter as well. It must "sell" the member on the idea of paying his pledge. Under no circumstances should you use expressions which create unnecessary irritation and antagonism. Ordinarily, a short or medium-length letter will make a more effective presentation than a long-winded message.

Build a sustaining interest in church support by writing "thank you's" to members who pay their pledges promptly and regularly. These notes will keep alive a personal relationship between your church and those who support it with their financial means.

Courtesy Letters Always Pay

RUPERT HUGHES once observed that "all charming people have a talent for gratitude." Everybody likes to be thanked, and the members of your church are no exception. "Thank you" is a powerful phrase. To make a person feel that he is appreciated, that his work really counts, that someone has noticed his services, is to gain his good will.

You will write letters of various kinds, but nothing will yield quicker dividends than courtesy notes. Because they are unexpected, they have an added charm.

Your members receive many letters asking them for their support and co-operation, but very few thanking them for their response. So it comes as a pleasant surprise to them when you take the time and trouble to express your appreciation of their help.

Always say "Thank you" and "Congratulations"

There isn't anything compulsory about writing brief congratulatory notes. But they are always wise investments in human relations. Your letter is read with interest and is remembered—because the flavor lasts. So take the time to say "thank you" now and then to folks who do so much for you and your church.

Every day some of your members perform services of genuine value to your church. Perhaps last night several women prepared an excellent dinner for members of the board of Christian education. Today a man used his automobile to take a group of Boy Scouts from your church troop to a district meeting held in a near-by city. Five high school girls designed, mimeographed, and stapled the unique programs for the annual banquet of the men's Bible class last Wednesday. Even though you thanked the workers personally, there is still a fine opportunity for letters of thanks.

Here are a few letters which convince their recipients that their loyalty to the church is sincerely appreciated—letters that increase their sense of pride in having done something worth while for their church.

Thanks to loyal member

Dear Mrs. Thompson:

Do you remember when you became a member of Elmwood Presbyterian Church?

You have been a member of our Church for quite a number of years--to be exact, since 1921--and we deeply appreciate your loyalty and devotion.

At all times you have shown an enthusiastic interest in our Church and its activities.

This message, we hope, will convey to you something of the deep sense of gratitude we feel for all that you have done.

Cordially yours,

Thanks to chairman of ushers

Dear Mr. Rayburn:

I want to thank you again for everything you did as chairman of our church ushers during the past year.

Your splendid work as head of this important committee added much to the effectiveness of our worship services. Thank you, too, for the mimeographed pamphlet listing the duties and responsibilities of ushers. It was timely, informative, and of great value.

We deeply appreciate your contributing so much to this important phase of our church program.

Sincerely yours,

Thanks to speakers

Dear Mrs. Armstrong:

Heartiest congratulations on your excellent talk, "Christian Hope in a Troubled World," which was given at the annual Day of Prayer program last Monday.

I have heard many fine compliments on your talk. It was informative, timely, and highly inspirational. Certainly it was a vital religious experience for all who had the pleasure of hearing you.

Sincerely yours,

~ ~ ~

Dear Mr. Blackburn:

This is just a note to thank you for the splendid talk on "After High School--What?" which you gave to our young people at their meeting Sunday night.

Everything you said--the stories you told of youths you had known, your discussion of modern trends in vocational guidance, your presentation of qualities necessary in facing life today --all this, and more, made a deep impression on all who heard you.

94

We appreciate your taking the time to contribute so much of value to our young people.

Sincerely yours,

Thanks for outstanding work

Dear Mrs. Franklin:

Never in my work as a minister have I seen such a complete and interesting report as the one you have prepared for the Women's Society of Christian Service for 19--.

Undoubtedly you spent many hours in gathering the information and many more in compiling it in such an excellent way.

This year's program was one of the best we have ever had, and its success was due in large measure to the many contributions which you made.

You have the gratitude of all church officers, as well as my deep personal appreciation, for your excellent work.

Cordially yours,

~　~　~

Dear Mrs. Meacham:

This is just a word to tell you how much I have appreciated your good work as a member of the Visitation Committee during the past year.

Through your unselfish service and that of other members of your committee, scores of persons have been brought into the brotherhood and fellowship of our Church.

You have my gratitude for your highly worthwhile service.

Sincerely yours,

Dear John:

Thank you very much for writing the excellent letter which we shall use in collecting delinquent pledges. It is courteous, compact, and interesting, and I am quite certain that it will be most resultful.

Miss Parkhurst started typing the letters this morning, and in a few days we shall see the results of your message. To me, your letter is one of the finest of its kind I have ever seen in church financial programs. I am certain that it will accomplish its objective.

Thank you again for your interest and help.

Sincerely yours,

~ ~ ~

Dear Mr. Longstreet:

Heartiest congratulations on your remarkable record of serving as teacher of the Men's Bible Class for twelve years.

Long before coming here as pastor, I had heard of your effective work as teacher of this fine class. And since being in Middletown I have had opportunity to see at first hand the magnificent way you serve as teacher. It is a high compliment to you that the class continues to grow and is now one of the largest in the state.

On behalf of our Church, I thank you sincerely for your loyal service.

Sincerely yours,

~ ~ ~

Dear Allen:

You are certainly to be congratulated on the fine showing of our boys at the recent district meeting of young people held in Dallas. Winning second place in a regional leadership contest is a splendid honor.

Without your interest and coaching, I am certain that our group would not have placed so high. It was especially gratifying to me that our boys placed first in the forensic events.

When I heard the results of the contest I immediately realized what a remarkable job you had done in view of your heavy loss of talent through graduation last May.

Best wishes to you for an equally successful year in 19--.

Cordially yours,

~ ~ ~

Dear Miss Fuston:

Congratulations to you and the cast in presenting the drama "Plate Passing in Reverse" at the church Wednesday night.

It was a worth-while production, and every member of the cast gave an excellent portrayal. All of us appreciate your hard work in making the production such an outstanding success.

You will be interested to know that receipts from the performance totaled more than $300. This amount gave our organ fund a big boost and now it looks as though we may be able to purchase one within the next two months.

Thank you again for your magnificent work.

Cordially yours,

~ ~ ~

Dear Miss Butler:

Heartiest congratulations on the most excellent program given recently by the Youth Choir!

I want you to know that we are proud of you, especially since you are keeping the organization functioning on its usual high plane during these busy days.

Congratulations on a job well done, and very best wishes to you.

Cordially yours,

~ ~ ~

Dear Mr. Garnett:

Thank you so much for your help in the construction of the Nativity scene which was placed in the hall near the opening of the sanctuary during the Christmas Season.

Members of our Church and visitors alike were thrilled at the beauty of the display. Indeed, many said it was the most impressive they had ever seen.

The display was most effective, due in large measure to the help you gave us.

Sincerely yours,

~ ~ ~

Dear Wesley:

You know, I've seen hundreds of church highway signs in my day, but the ones you made for us are by far the most attractive that I've seen.

They are splendid and will certainly be noticed by hundreds of motorists along the main highways in and out of our city. I especially liked your lettering, which is dignified and highly readable.

We know that these "highway messengers" will show results in attracting countless travelers to our Church.

Congratulations and thanks for a job well done!

Cordially yours,

Dear Walter:

Thank you very much for your advice and counsel at our meeting with the painting contractors Wednesday afternoon. I especially appreciated your suggestions regarding the new color scheme for the sanctuary.

Painters will begin work next Monday morning, and soon the interior of our church will be "spic and span" again.

Thank you again for your help.

Sincerely yours,

Congratulations on completing church course

Dear Mrs. Carson:

You are to be congratulated on successfully completing your work in the recent school of instruction.

I have unqualified admiration for anyone who shows such interest and ability. I feel that you have every right to be proud of your achievement and that with your additional training you will prove even more valuable as a teacher in our Church School.

No one has ever done her work more capably or conscientiously than you, and we appreciate it very much.

Cordially yours,

~   ~   ~

Dear George:

Very few church leaders complete their first-year training courses with a scholastic average of 94. In doing so, you have made a remarkable record and established an excellent standard for your remaining courses.

I congratulate you upon your fine record and wish you every success in maintaining it during the years ahead.

Cordially yours,

Thanks for a party

Dear Mr. and Mrs. Harris:

Parties may come and parties may go, but the one you had Thursday night for members of the choir was an unforgettable occasion.

Wasn't Bill Bryant's impersonation of me a scream? And wasn't Ethel Buntin's parody a clever act? But the most memorable thing to all of us was your gracious hospitality.

In several churches in which I have served, choir members are "unsung heroes." Too often we take for granted the many fine contributions of a choir to a church. But not you two grand people.

All of us had a wonderful time and we want you to know how much we appreciate your kindness.

Cordially yours,

Thanks for gracious acts

Dear Mrs. Lucas:

Your donation of cookies to the Sunday evening "Eat-a-Bite" program for young people is deeply appreciated. Your cookies were delicious--so much so that several of the girls said they were going to call you and get the recipe.

All those in attendance join with me in thanking you for your help in making the affair a success. And we thank you, too, for furnishing all the materials and work and time that went into the cookies.

Cordially yours,

~ ~ ~

Dear Mrs. Batchelor:

Thank you so much for the beautiful flowers which you sent to the sanctuary last Sunday. Many members told me how your bouquet added to the beauty of the service.

You'll be glad to know that after the services Sunday night Mr. Bartlett took the flowers to the City Hospital where they will bring cheer to the patients.

I'm sure that everyone--both those who attended church Sunday and those at the hospital--would join me in thanking you for your kindness.

Cordially yours,

No courtesy letter is worth the paper on which it is written unless it is sincere and genuine. Even when the letter will go to twenty-five persons who served on a committee, make it sound like a personal message. Give the reader the satisfaction of feeling that he is appreciated as an individual —that your letter was written to him. Write more courtesy notes, make them "ring" with genuineness and sincerity, and you'll be amazed how they will strengthen cordial relationships.

101

Cordial Contacts with Youth

G EARING church activities to the needs and interests of
youth is no easy task. Wise pastors know that young
people have a stake in what is done in their churches, that
they have a lot to give in the way of practical ingenuity,
enthusiasm, and service; that they are partners in church
affairs—and justifiably refuse to remain silent partners.

Getting a young person interested in religion is one thing,
but keeping that youth sold on the church and its program
is even more important. Young persons, perhaps more than
any other group in the church, need a sustained interest to
keep their devotion alive.

Hundreds of young persons turn away from religion.
Why? Perhaps they feel that the youth program does not
have enough variety. They may believe that their participation in church activities doesn't particularly matter—that
they can drop out and never be missed. Some of them turn
away from religion because they view it as a pious, long-
faced experience. In some instances adult leaders tend to
become "bosses" rather than friends and counselors. Whatever the reason for the young people's alienation, each pastor seeks to improve his relationship with the youths of his
church.

Ultimately, the success or failure of the young people's
program lies with the minister. Devoted and competent

though they may be, no Sunday school teaching staff, no director of religious education, no associate pastor can substitute for the minister. His is a unique responsibility. Only by sharing a personal companionship with youth can the minister be certain that assured and accredited values can be transmitted to the oncoming generation.

The pastor's best means of keeping in direct contact with young persons is by being "one of them"—by making their problems his own. He will then be able to help each one in growing into Christian maturity. At the same time, he can use all possible channels of communication—telephone, news sheets, bulletins, and letters—in keeping alive their interest and co-operation.

Youth wants attention

Young persons, being quite human—though quite confused at times—naturally enjoy and appreciate individual attention. They like to know that their pastor and church are interested in them, not in the realm of religious affairs alone, but in their "outside" activities and interests.

Every cordial contact made by a personal letter to a young person strengthens the church of tomorrow. So the message you write to a youth today has cumulative value; it will pay dividends to the church now, and many years from now.

Letters of this sort need not be long; in fact, a note of six or eight lines will make its recipient feel that his progress is being followed with interest. In all likelihood the letter will spur him to greater efforts and will increase his loyalty toward the church.

Here are examples of congratulatory notes to young people that pay enormous dividends in terms of good will.

Congratulations for honors earned

Dear Bill:

Please accept my hearty congratulations on the many high honors you have attained in Boy Scout work. It was a thrilling moment for all of us when you became an Eagle Scout at the meeting last Tuesday night.

Your record is unusually remarkable because of your school work and also because of your duties in serving as a carrier for the Dallas "Morning News" for years.

I am sure that all your friends join with me in wishing you continued success.

Sincerely yours,

~　~　~

Dear Ted:

The pleasantest piece of news I've heard in a long time is that you have been elected chairman of the recreation committee of the Wesley Foundation. It's a great opportunity, and I'm sure that you will make the most of it.

You're going to have a fine group to work with, and with your background and experience I am certain that your program will be one of the most outstanding we've ever had.

Your enthusiasm and ability are just what the Foundation needs in its recreation affairs. You will do a grand job. If there is anything I can do to help, you can rely on me.

Sincerely yours,

~　~　~

Dear Bruce:

I was happy to see your name in the Norman "Transcript" as a member of the 19-- All-Central Conference high school football team. Your selection for this honor is a fitting climax to your splendid record in football.

Even more of a credit to you than inclusion on the team of all-stars is the fine brand of sportsmanship you have displayed so consistently throughout the three years of competition.

I am sure you will play the more important game of life with the same enthusiasm and the same sportsmanship, and I have no doubt that you will be equally successful at it.

Sincerely yours,

~ ~ ~

Dear Lucille:

Though I knew of your leadership ability from your fine work in our Church, I did not know of your writing talent until I saw the current number of "Central Hi-Lights."

This is an excellent school newspaper, and certainly your article was one of its most outstanding features. You have a highly readable way of expressing yourself, a trait which characterizes all successful writers.

Congratulations and best wishes.

Cordially yours,

~ ~ ~

Dear Madeline:

Good news travels fast! I have just heard of your remarkable achievement in receiving the Mothers' Association award as the most outstanding student at G--- University.

Again you have demonstrated your ability "to do all things well," a trait which characterized your many activities here at Central Church.

Your many friends here join with me in extending heartiest congratulations.

Sincere good wishes and the best of luck to you.

Cordially yours,

~ ~ ~

Dear Maurice:

Just a few words to tell you how glad I was to hear that you have been elected president of the high school boys' glee club.

Your achievement is the best possible recognition of your loyal and efficient service to the organization. I am happy for you in your success.

Sincerely yours,

~ ~ ~

Dear Rosalyn:

Good for you! I have just learned that you won the medal presented by the Pioneer Music Club.

So I am writing these few words to congratulate you upon a real honor--one that speaks highly for your all-round musical ability and personality.

Keep up the good work, and the best of luck to you.

Cordially yours,

Dear Roy:

CONGRATULATIONS!

I have just heard that you have received a special certificate for a perfect attendance record of twelve years in the Simpsonville Public Schools.

Twelve years of perfect attendance is an accomplishment to be proud of, Roy, and I want to congratulate you upon this remarkable achievement.

You have my sincere best wishes for every success in the years ahead.

Sincerely yours,

Thanks for services well done

Dear Walter:

Thank you so much for helping us last Sunday in delivering baskets of food, clothing, and toys to the needy of our city.

I'm sure that your Christmas was a brighter one because you showed the true spirit of the occasion by bringing happiness to others.

You'll agree with one of the other boys when he declared: "Now I really know the meaning of the phrase 'Inasmuch as ye have done it unto one of the least of these my brethren, ye have done it unto me.'"

You have my gratitude for your loyal service.

Cordially yours,

~ ~ ~

Dear Mary Evelyn:

Congratulations on the splendid way in which you served as toastmistress at the annual choir banquet Tuesday night.

You presided with perfection, of course, and your clever imitations of the different types of choir members really brought down the house.

Since your part of the occasion was done so well, I wanted to compliment you and tell you how much we all enjoyed it.

Very sincerely yours,

~ ~ ~

Dear Rollo:

Sunday night's performance of "Who Is My Neighbor?" by the Young People's Drama Club was one of the finest religious plays I have ever witnessed. One of the factors which made it so effective was the splendid way in which you played the part of the beggar.

All who attended the program had a great lesson impressed upon them, and I am certain that the play's influence will be felt in the lives of all who attended.

Since your part in the presentation was so well done, I wanted to compliment you and thank you for your large part in the success of the program.

Cordially yours,

Starting today, be on the alert for opportunities to write friendly letters of encouragement to youth. Such letters are written far too seldom, for in many churches no one considers this important public relations challenge a part of his job. If your letter is well written, the favorable impression which it creates will endure. In fact, in no other area of church administration can you achieve such lasting loyalty for such a small investment. Through counsel and companionship, through personal contacts and letters, assist your young people to grow "in wisdom and stature, and in favor with God and man."

Pouring Oil on Troubled Waters

A S THE key person in the administrative program of his church, the pastor is automatically assumed to be "Mr. Fixit" when negative circumstances arise. No matter how high the degree of operating efficiency in his church, misunderstandings and dissatisfactions are certain to occur. Most of the time, the task of straightening out the inevitable "kinks" falls on the pastor's shoulders.

Every parish has its critics. "In almost all churches," observed John Timothy Stone, president of the Presbyterian Theological Seminary, "there are those members who for one reason or another are out of sympathy with the church and who do not hesitate to express ill will or grievance when the opportunity affords."

In addition to cases of specific complaint about major areas of church programs, the minister usually falls heir to the delicate task of answering grievances incurred in many relationships sometimes far removed from direct activities of his work in his parish.

If the heating system fails to function efficiently in the sanctuary, it is the pastor who usually takes the brunt of the criticism. If little Lucy Van Swiggle isn't invited to her Sunday School class party, the minister must listen to her worried parents. It is a rare day when he does not face enough complaints and suggestions to exhaust the average man. His "bosses" can sometimes be numbered by the total membership of his church.

Diplomacy always pays

By virtue of his position, the pastor must have the talents of a diplomat so that he can iron out difficulties and regain good will if it has been jeopardized. To be sure, he can solve many human complications through personal contacts and by telephone, but he can often utilize letters in "pouring oil on troubled waters."

First of all, in writing a letter of this sort you should answer the complaint promptly. Even if you cannot give a definite decision immediately, you can write a brief note expressing regret for the cause of the complaint, and assuring the person that prompt action will be taken.

Use the opening paragraph to get in step with the reader. This may be done by thanking him for his inquiry or utterance, expressing regret for the occurrence (if the situation justifies it), assuring him that the difficulty will be corrected, or using some other point on which you can agree with him. You see at once how such an opening disarms the reader and puts him in a receptive mood.

Show the reader that you appreciate his point of view. Avoid phrases like "I cannot understand" or "I am at a loss to know." These expressions are likely to antagonize him at a time when he is already irritated. Other words and phrases which tend to provoke are: "you claim," "you state," "you assert," and "your complaint."

Emphasize the positive

Always emphasize the positive, constructive side of the adjustment problem. Avoid the use of certain words which suggest unpleasant experiences to the reader. Stress the future—what will be done—rather than the past difficulty.

Some of the complaints and suggestions which come to you will be so discourteous, sarcastic, and ridiculous that you may be tempted to reply in the same tone. But you must never show irritation, however much the circumstance may seem to justify it. Indeed, you must remain calm and courteous if your letter is to build good will and understanding. "A soft answer turneth away wrath" and "grievous words stir up anger."

Even if the person is wrong, don't tell him so point-blank. Instead, express courtesy in the opening paragraph and thus pave the way for friendly feelings. Throughout the letter take the view that the reader is benefiting you by his complaint or criticism. If you are wrong, admit the error at once without unnecessary apology, but with proper expression of regret for the difficulty. In every instance use persuasion rather than argument.

For the most part, don't use the excuse that the mistake is a fault of a member of the church staff. Avoid such phrases as "the trouble was caused by our new custodian, who is unfamiliar with our kitchen facilities." Try to avoid the statement that "this error will never happen again." In closing the letter, do not suggest future disappointments by saying, "I certainly hope that we won't give you any more trouble."

Write effective endings

Close your letter with a positive thought. Note the following effective endings:

> It gives us pleasure to help you.

> We shall be grateful for your understanding, your forgiveness, and your assistance.

> Thank you for bringing the matter to my attention.

111

If there are any further questions, please let me know.

We are sorry for this error, and thank you for calling it to our attention.

Thank you for giving me the opportunity to explain this matter.

Now let's look at some letters which embody tactfulness of expression in dealing positively and constructively with situations which are essentially negative:

Dear Mrs. Spears:

I understand how disappointing it must have been to discover that the hymnal which you gave to the Church in memory of your parents was not among the new books used for the first time last Sunday.

Before delivering the first shipment of memorial plates last Saturday, the printer informed us that he would withhold the remaining ones until the ink had dried. But today we received the other plates, including the one listing your parents' names. So we shall have all hymnals ready for use in the sanctuary before next Sunday.

Thank you for calling this to our attention.

Sincerely yours,

~ ~ ~

My dear Mr. Galt:

You had every right to be annoyed when you received two reminders requesting action on your church pledge which was paid December 14, and we are sorry indeed that the mistake occurred.

To be frank, this is exactly the truth--Dan Cupid has been one of the busiest workers in our church office this fall, with the

112

result that three secretaries were married. With three changes in personnel, naturally our system of records was for a time not as efficient as we like for it to be. But I am glad to say that everything is now running smoothly again.

Thank you for your letter. We appreciate your reporting to us, with such understanding, a situation which must have been puzzling to you.

Sincerely yours,

~ ~ ~

Dear Mr. Felgar:

You were quite right to call my attention to the noise created by children running through the halls of the church last Wednesday afternoon when funeral services were being conducted.

As far as I can learn, most of the boys arrived at the church at least fifteen minutes before the weekly meeting of their Boy Scout troop. They came in the side entrance and were not aware of the services in the sanctuary. You will remember that an usher left the services and talked to the boys. All of them expressed regret and were profoundly sorry for the disturbance.

Thank you for giving me the opportunity to explain this incident.

Sincerely yours,

~ ~ ~

Dear Mrs. Huckaby:

You will never know how embarrassed I was to discover that we had omitted Betty's name from the list of high school seniors published in last Sunday's bulletin.

113

Every item of copy is edited carefully and then the proofs are checked. While we try to keep mistakes at a minimum, once in a while some seemingly preventable error occurs. When it does, of course, we are anxious to correct it.

Please tell Betty that we are running a correction in next Sunday's bulletin.

Thank you for bringing the matter to my attention.

Cordially yours,

~ ~ ~

Dear Mr. McKowen:

Thank you for your letter of November 10.

We would be delighted to keep the church gymnasium open five nights a week, and are looking forward to the time when we can do so again. But with conditions as they are at present, we can open it only on Monday nights.

As you know, we have recently found it impossible to hire an adult to supervise activities of young persons using the gymnasium. We have tried to use volunteers, but this plan has proved unsatisfactory.

As we're sure you understand what we are up against, we are confident you will be patient with us until we can again open the gymnasium five nights each week--and we do hope that time isn't far off, for we should like immensely to make it available to our young people.

Cordially yours,

~ ~ ~

Dear Mrs. Snead:

You are exactly right! We should have called you about the meeting of the missions committee.

In these busy times (fourteen meetings were held at the church last week) something goes wrong once in a while, despite our earnest efforts to keep all church activities functioning efficiently.

We know that from time to time we make mistakes and if these were not called to our attention, we should not be able to correct our errors and prevent a recurrence. That is why we appreciate your letter.

We apologize for the disappointment we caused, and assure you that ours was the greater loss, for we certainly need and want your help in our mission work--and intend to call on you for future meetings.

Sincerely yours,

~ ~ ~

Dear Mrs. Brookes:

Is my face red?

After writing you as I did in my letter of January 12, and giving you what I thought to be the correct facts, I am very much embarrassed to note my mistake.

Your pledge to the World Service Fund was paid December 28. In checking through our cards we did not find your receipt with your card. Yesterday we found it, and your records have now been corrected.

We're terribly sorry about the error--especially so since you have always been so generous in supporting the World Service programs.

Thank you for calling our attention to this mistake.

Sincerely yours,

115

Dear Mr. Kolb:

Thank you for writing and giving us the opportunity to explain why we decided to join with congregations of four other churches at the evening union services in the University Amphitheater during July and August.

As you probably know, the decision for us to join with other churches in union services again this summer was made by the Board of Stewards at its last meeting.

Board members felt that since our attendance at night services during the two hot months is usually quite small, it would be better to participate in the outdoor services. And, too, because of the beauty and coolness of the amphitheater, they knew it would be a delightful place for worship and, at the same time, for fellowship with our friends from other churches.

We hope you will consider these to be good reasons for our decision, and will help us to make the community worship services successful.

Cordially yours,

Regardless of who is at fault, be sure to indicate at the very beginning of your letter that you are not averse to receiving complaints and criticisms. Instead, show the complainant that you regard his grievance as an opportunity to serve him. Show him that, whether he is right or wrong, you will be glad to explain or investigate the matter. Make every knock a boost. Solve each problem thoughtfully, patiently, and gracefully. Finally, remember that "he that ruleth his spirit [is better] than he that taketh a city."

CHAPTER 11

Building Loyalty by Letter

EVERY church is a comradeship of worship and service. If members of your congregation are to be associated in a quest for the highest spiritual ends, you must keep them busy and interested. There, in a nutshell, is one of the "musts" of a successful ministry.

How can you create a greater degree of loyalty? What is your responsibility in arousing devotion and interest in your congregation? Success is dependent on numerous factors. But easily one of the most important elements is to improve your ability as an interpreter, a master salesman, of the greatest values in the world.

Every successful person, and especially a leader, must be a salesman. This vital fact was emphasized by Charles M. Schwab when he said: "Many of us think of salesmen as people traveling around with sample kits. Instead we are all salesmen, every day of our lives. We are selling our ideas, our plans, our energies, our enthusiasm to those with whom we come in contact."

But today's sales manager does not make calls, ring doorbells, and get all the orders. He instructs his salesmen and inspires them to do their best—then they go out after business. You as a minister can increase your administrative ability and enlarge your staff by training more people in the tasks of your church and then putting them to work.

The pastor as coach

Judson J. McKim, for many years general secretary of the Cincinnati Y. M. C. A., and also a minister, once remarked that a pastor can be most helpful to his people by thinking of himself as the coach or professional engineer in developing religious programs. He believed that often good minds and skills existing in the church are inhibited by the minister's failure to tap the latent resources existing within his organization.

We must never forget that Christianity started with laymen. Neither Jesus nor any of his disciples were members of the priesthood or the clergy. And as Harry Emerson Fosdick has reminded us, "In every accent of Jesus' teaching he brushes past the languages of the schools to deal in plain speech with the areas where laymen and laywomen live and work." Certainly no pastor can really doubt the Master's ability to bring out the possibilities of average men and women.

How can the interests, abilities, and enthusiasm of church members be co-ordinated and unified into a successful program? Certainly such utilization of talents requires time, thought, patience, vision, and executive ability.

First of all, remember that members of your congregation are no different from other persons whom you meet along the street every day. Like leaves, no two are alike. And yet they have the same longings and desires as other people. They respond to the same psychological reactions. And above all, remember that every person, without exception —even though outward evidence is often to the contrary— has at least one talent which can be invested for the Kingdom.

Increasing church loyalty

Whiting Williams says that the dominating motive of men is "the wish for worth," the longing to feel that they are essential to something or someone. Make your members feel that they do count for something, that what they do is important—just as the Master did so often—and you have strengthened their loyalty to the church.

But you can never hold the loyalty of people by admitting them into the church and then giving them nothing to do. To be left idle leaves the impression of being unappreciated. "I had rather be a doorkeeper in the house of my God . . ." is more than a phrase from the Bible. It is an inner appreciation of worth which keeps a person going.

Somehow, many church members have the idea that some expertness in theology is a prerequisite to religious effectiveness. This feeling of spiritual inadequacy prevents many laymen from taking their places in the more vital phases of the church program.

Even though you may emphasize loyalty on special occasions throughout the year, you face the daily problem of keeping your congregation interested and also growing into spiritual maturity. No church has ever succeeded without the constant loyalty and devotion of its members. Loyalty isn't a quality reserved exclusively for special occasions but one which must be in operation in all phases of church life at all times.

Use letters regularly

Many and varied are the methods used by today's pastor in deepening the spiritual life of members of his church. But whatever procedures he follows, he can augment the enlistment of his members in the consecration of their time, talent, and money to the Kingdom of God through the regular use of effective letters.

Naturally, you will make regular contact with innumerable persons through conferences, interviews, telephone conversations, group meetings, worship services, and many other media. But in addition to all of those, you can greatly expand your ministry through the use of effective letters. Personal letters are best, of course, because they are tremendously worth while in cementing members' loyalty and maintaining their active support. But you may also use well-written form letters done in a personalized fashion. In fact, you should use both kinds in strengthening the ties of church loyalty. Results? There will be many of incalculable value, both immediate and cumulative.

Types of letters which may be utilized are as numerous as the activities and objectives of a church. Some of the typical themes are worship, attendance, fellowship, finance, prayer, stewardship, sacraments, special programs, and leadership.

Of course all the letters in this book are in a broad sense loyalty builders, and the "unnecessary" courtesy letters in Chapter 8 are excellent loyalty builders of a specialized sort. The following specimens further illustrate the effective use of personal and form letters in building loyalty, devotion, co-operation, and harmony.

To new church members

Dear Mr. and Mrs. Jones:

You are among our newer members. We are happy and proud to have you. As pastor I wish I could drop around and see you every week. But in a large church that is impossible. But if you need me by reason of sickness or trouble please give me a ring.

We want Johnson Memorial Church to help you every week. Millions receive a steady supply of strength from the habit of regular church attendance. Life today has its worries. The hymns of the church, the reading of the Bible in church, the uplifting sermons--all these can help each of us.

I beg you, and all other members, to be in God's house every Sunday. Please bring someone with you. Help bring another person into the membership of the Church.

Sermon Sunday morning: "Saboteurs of Character." Sermon Sunday evening: "The Man Who Was Thrilled by Religion."

"And the hour shall be filled with music,
With worship, and song, and prayer;
And the burden of life shall be lifted
From all who enter there."

Most cordially yours,[1]

~ ~ ~

Dear Mr. and Mrs. Smith:

On behalf of the Session of our Church I am very glad to express our pleasure that you have united with the Church and are now prepared to take an active and vital part in its work and worship.

I hope very much that the Church through its varied program may meet all of your spiritual needs and that you may find rich fellowship, joy, and inspiration through your participation.

You will find enclosed information cards which I would appreciate your completing and returning to the church office as soon as is convenient for you.

[1] Used by Rolla S. Kenaston, minister Johnson Memorial Methodist Church, Huntington, W. Va.

121

There is also enclosed for your information a copy of this year's budget of the Church and cards on which you may indicate the extent to which you feel able to share in it. I trust that you will give this matter serious thought and that you will wish to share as generously as possible in the wide program and opportunities of the Church. You may return the pledge cards to the budget secretary,_____ at _____, at your convenience.

Once again, welcome to our membership and may God's blessing attend you in our fellowship together.

Sincerely yours,

Clerk of the Session [2]

~ ~ ~

Dear Mrs. Smith:

We were so happy to receive you formally into the Church on Sunday morning. We offer you now our hearts, our fellowship, our prayers, our service.

The members of the staff want you to know that anything we can do to enrich your life, to help you in emergencies, to assist you to a richer fellowship with God, we shall be glad to do.

May I suggest that where possible, you associate with the various activities of the Church--Church School classes, the mid-week meetings, the Woman's Society of Christian Service. There you will have opportunity to become acquainted with others in the Church and render the service of which you are uniquely capable.

[2] Used by Harry Bertrand Taylor, pastor First Presbyterian Church, Syracuse, N. Y.

Will you not pray for us in our work, that we may be guided in these critical days in all our plans and labors?

May God bless you.

Sincerely yours,[3]

~ ~ ~

Dear Friend:

It is our great privilege to extend to you on behalf of the Session and the Board of Trustees a very cordial welcome to the fellowship of this Church.

Membership naturally carries some responsibilities which, we trust, you may wish to share with us.

All the activities of our Church are supported by the free-will offerings of the people. To contribute to this support, in just proportion, is not only an obligation, but also an act of worship.

A pledge card is enclosed, which we request you to sign. It may be placed on the offering plate next Sunday, or mailed to the church office. The loose offerings are for the Session Fund, and are not used to meet the current expenses of the Church.

We sincerely trust that you may find your new church home congenial in every way. It is our custom to send out this letter to our new members so that they may have the opportunity to enter into the fullness of privilege from the very beginning. On receipt of your pledge, envelopes will be sent to you. If you prefer to pay quarterly, a statement will be mailed to you at the beginning of each quarter in advance.

[3] Albert Edward Day, minister First Methodist Church, Pasadena, Calif.

Enclosed is a booklet which lists our various church organizations and activities. We trust you will affiliate yourself with some of these groups.

Sincerely yours,

Clerk of Session

Treasurer [4]

~ ~ ~

Dear Friend Audrey:

How happy we are to welcome you as a member of Centenary Tabernacle Methodist Church! We are sure you will remember the day you joined the Church with pride and joy all the days of your life.

The highest honor which can come to any of us is to be a part of the group of people who are carrying on Christ's work on the earth. You will remember this, won't you, and give your best to Him?

Give my kindest regards and best wishes to everyone at your house.

Sincerely yours,[5]

To a new teacher

Dear Miss Harlow:

We are delighted to welcome you as a new teacher in our Sunday School.

[4] Used by Stuart Nye Hutchison, pastor East Liberty Presbyterian Church, Pittsburgh, Pa.

[5] Everett W. Palmer, pastor Centenary Tabernacle Methodist Church, Camden, N. J.

You will be of inestimable help in increasing our Church School attendance, and more important, in making Sunday School instruction of value in building human life into the image of God.

Through our recently adopted plans we hope that every child within the families and constituents of our Church will be drawn into the educational program. It is good to know that you will help us in reaching this high goal.

My best wishes go with you as you begin what I hope will be a most profitable and pleasant work. If I can ever be of assistance to you, please let me know and I shall gladly do so.

Sincerely yours,

To new committee members

Dear Mr. Moats:

We are delighted to welcome you as a member of the Greeters' Committee for the year.

Through you and other members of the committee we want to convince everyone that the "WELCOME" on our outdoor bulletin board is a real flesh-and-blood affair with warm and hearty cordiality.

Yours is a high responsibility. You are the "contact man" —the first person worshipers will see when they come to worship each Sunday. Our services will be brightened and warmed for all who come our way because of your cordial welcome to them.

Your generous and constant help is deeply appreciated.

Sincerely yours,

~ ~ ~

Dear Mrs. Hawkins:

It is my good pleasure to inform you of your appointment to the music committee. Nothing is more vital in our Church than the ministry of music, and I am certain that you will cooperate with us by serving on this important committee.

Briefly, the duties of your committee are (1) to attend choir rehearsals when convenient, (2) to provide music and other appropriate equipment, (3) to set up the item for music in the budget of the Church, and (4) to counsel with the choir director and organist.

Since you understand so well what good music can do for the spiritual life of our Church, we know you can be of inestimable help to us.

Cordially yours,

To a newly baptized boy

Dear John:

Along with this letter goes your certificate of baptism. And I want to tell you how glad I am to have become acquainted with you through the service of baptism. I have always liked little boys very much, and knowing you does not make me like them any less!

I like little boys because I know they are going to grow up some day; and when you were christened I was thinking that since your father and mother were making some very significant promises to God about you, and since the Church prayed that you would become a Christian man, that your future looked pretty bright.

Since you have now become a preparatory member of the Church, I do want you to know that there is a tremendously warm place at the heart of the Church for you. And in the future if there is anything I can do for your father or mother or for you to help you achieve a Christian boyhood in a joyous Christian home, please let me know.

Your friend, [6]

[6] Robert Leonard Tucker, pastor First Methodist Church, New Haven, Conn.

On prayer

Dear Friends:

Christmas Evans, the noted Welsh preacher, once stated that "prayer is the rope up in the belfry; we pull it and it rings the bell up in heaven." To know that the bell rings and that its music can flood our lives is a great comfort to all of us.

Great personalites of all ages have been strengthened by prayer. Martin Luther, when faced with the gigantic tasks of his life, said: "I have so much to do that I cannot get along without three hours a day of praying." Sir Matthew Hale declared: "If I omit praying and reading God's word in the morning, nothing goes right all day." General Havelock, we are told, arose at four if the hour of marching was six, rather than miss the precious privilege of communing with God before starting the day. These men, as have all faithful Christians, found great comfort in prayer.

Humanly enough, we often pray for ourselves as individuals. But we must expand our prayer life and think of others--not just those around us, but God's people all over the world.

To be sure, we are living in a hurried age. Everything has been speeded up. The immediacy of things demands our time and attention. But because life is like that today, we need prayer all the more. It is a reservoir of strength and courage. It gives life a unity and direction.

The rope to the bell is close by. But the bell can never ring itself. Let us pull the rope! Let us give prayer a vital place in our lives! Let us use it more, and the heavenly music will fill our lives with sweet melodies of peace and joy. Why don't you ring?

Cordially yours,

127

On being happy

Dear Friend:

A colored man at Colonel Clark's mission in Chicago said: "Bredren, when I gets to de gates of hebben, if dey shuts me out, I'll say, 'Anyhow, I hadda good time gettin' here!'"

Traveling the highways of life can be a happy experience. Sanctimoniousness doesn't necessarily indicate saintliness. Real religion isn't a false smile which you "turn on" for special occasions. It's deeper than that. It's an inner courage and faith which are radiated--even in adversity.

Those who neither sing nor hum are out of tune with the infinite. You know, I've always thought that a pessimist in the church is as much out of place as a pickle in a freezer of ice cream.

Christianity is the highest source of joy. It is not religion, but the lack of it, that makes people unhappy. "The fruit of the Spirit is love, joy, peace." "Rejoice in the Lord always: and again I say, rejoice." "Believing, ye rejoice with joy unspeakable and full of glory." Let's remember that it is our duty to be joyful and our privilege to spread joy among others.

Cordially yours,

For the new year

Dear Friend:

NINETEEN FORTY-FIVE . . .

. . . has joined the parade of past years. All of us have had our disappointments and successes. But we should be thankful for our share of good health, good will, and sincere friendship.

Looking back over the year, I am deeply grateful to you who have shown your loyalty toward the Church. You recognize the

128

importance of keeping spiritual values alive and the worth of staying in tune with the highest.

May the New Year, which is just starting, bring you and yours the best of everything.

The single purpose of this letter is to tell you how much your co-operation and prayers have meant to me--and to send you a real old-fashioned wish for a Happy New Year in 1946!

Sincerely yours,

~ ~ ~

Dear Friends:

19-- is just around the corner!

There is a great deal of speculation and uncertainty about what the new year has in store for us.

It is not possible to "look into the crystal ball" and come up with the answers to the many perplexing problems facing all of us--but we do know that our Church must meet many challenges in the months ahead.

Here is where all of you enter the picture.

How fine it would be if everyone in our Church would make the resolution to put God and the Church first in everything next year. Our lives would be blessed and our Church would go forward in new achievements.

You will have an opportunity to repledge your loyalty and love toward the Church at the morning services Sunday, January 7. Please come. I shall be expecting you.

Cordially yours,

Dear Mrs. Barker:

The dawn of the new year brings a welcome opportunity to express our appreciation for your fine services throughout the year just closed.

Our Church made marvelous progress in many areas during the last year, and much of it was due to the loyal support given by people like you.

As we look forward to the coming year, it is my hope that the best of everything will be yours.

Sincerely yours,

For the new church year

Dear Member of First Church:

I am happy to note that you are one of the sustaining members of our Church. In plain words, you and a company of friends of like mind and spirit, support the Church. You help make this Church a going and growing organization.

As we enter upon the new conference year we want the co-operation of all--in every way possible. Three things stand out as major objectives:

1) We desire personal loyalty to Christ as Lord and Master--a loyalty acknowledged in life and in deed, in worship and in work. Let us be simple and sincere followers of our Lord every day!

2) We wish to be broad-minded and sympathetic toward all churches and all welfare organizations, but we believe that our first love and principal devotion should be for our own. A man appreciates other men's families most when he loves and supports his own!

3) We believe that a member in the pew--regularly-- on Sundays, is worth two or a dozen in some remote place but

130

with us "in spirit." A church-going people makes a mighty church and a potent preacher! Such folks generally subscribe--and <u>pay</u>. They know what the church program is--and help carry it out. They constitute the real force; the others too frequently become the field!

As your pastor I send you cordial greetings and challenge your best interest and fidelity.

In our Master's Name,

Very sincerely,

P. S. Sunday School every Sunday through the summer at 9:30 A.M.; Public Worship with sermon, 10:45 A.M. And as for your financial support--DO IT WEEKLY! [7]

For Holy Week

An Invitation

This is Holy Week.

For some who read these lines it will never come again on earth. Every year sees the passing from our community of someone whose going away leaves a lonely place that no one else can fill.

Some take the great adventure into the unknown without having made a commitment of their souls to their Heavenly Father, without having given youth the wholesome example of publicly affirming their allegiance to Jesus Christ.

Next Sunday is Easter. The ministers of the Baptist and Methodist churches in Sidney Center will gladly welcome at the altar of the Church those who are willing to take their stand for Christ and his way of life.

[7] Edward Burns Martin, pastor First Methodist Church, South Bend, Ind.

If you have never openly avowed your allegiance to Him and his cause there is no longer any need to postpone the day. Your relatives, your friends, and your neighbors will be glad to see you do it. Moreover, it is one step you will never regret taking. And too, it is a step that He has been hoping you will take.

Perhaps you have a friend to whom you would like to speak. Deep down in your heart you want him or her to be counted IN time and Eternity.

The greatest word on the clock of time is--NOW.

A special Union Service will be held in the Methodist Church, Friday evening at 7:30. The Rev. Gerald Jack will preach. This is your invitation to be there.[8]

For special drives

Hello There--

Do you mind if I pull up a chair? There's a good word I want to say to you.

It concerns the church on the corner of Fifth and Cooper.

Do you know that, despite handicaps which harass downtown industrial city churches most severely, Centenary Tabernacle is going ahead!

Its best days aren't in the past, splendid as that has been. They are in the NOW and in the years ahead.

For a church which draws membership and support from so far and wide as C. T. to maintain previous attendance

[8] Used by John Edwin Price, pastor, Methodist Church, Sidney Center, N. Y.

is quite a feat. But attendance this year, both at the morning and evening services, shows a marked increase over last year.

Then, too, there is Child Center, Inc. Every day, thirty or more little children are gathered in the arms of Christian love and care. That is being done because of this Church's will to obey the spirit of Jesus. The Center has a staff of five paid workers and a budget of approximately $10,000. It is becoming known as one of the best institutions of its kind in the state.

These are a few indications of what's going on at C. T.

I don't know what you think of it, but to me it's an honor to be a part of such a church.

Membership here gives opportunity for courage, vision, and high enterprise in the greatest work on earth, even that of Jesus Christ, the world's Redeemer!

I say we have good reason to celebrate an <u>Achievement Day</u>. And the time I set for this is Sunday, December 3.

Sincerely yours,[9]

~   ~   ~

Dear Church Member:

The announcement of CHURCH LOYALTY IN TRINITY CHURCH brings a host of pleasant memories. Large crowds, extra services, and good times. This year we want to add another element. Our slogan is "Let Loyalty Month be a Spiritual Blessing."

OUR STEWARDS will do their part. They expect to visit systematically every member on their list.

OUR PASTOR will try to visit every office and business in Tallahassee.

[9] Everett W. Palmer, minister Centenary Tabernacle Methodist Church, Camden, N. J.

OUR WOMEN are asked to join the "five and five" club, visiting five neighbors who are members of the Church, and five prospective members.

THE MEMBERS are asked to seek one hundred per cent attendance, attending at least one worship service every week. (Services at 9:00 A.M., 11:00 A.M., and 7:00 P.M. Sunday and 7:30 P.M. Wednesday.)

However much we come to church little good will be realized unless we come in the right spirit. Let us therefore:

BE THANKFUL. Thanksgiving month should be one of the happiest in the year. Think how much we have for which to be thankful.

BE HUMBLE AND REPENTANT, for we know how little we deserve what we have because of sin in our life.

BE CO-OPERATIVE. God may have a great task for some of us this month. Listen to Him, and be willing to work for and with Him.

Faithfully yours,

"LET LOYALTY MONTH BE A SPIRITUAL BLESSING TO YOU" [10]

~ ~ ~

My Dear Church Members and Friends:

The home is the foundation of society and is absolutely vital to the stability of both Church and State.

Public institutions serve a public need, but they fall far short of serving a personal one. Some time ago I heard a story

[10] Used by Jack Anderson, pastor Trinity Methodist Church Tallahassee, Fla.

of a lady who said: "I was born in a hospital; I was educated in a public school; I was married in a church. When I am hungry, I go to a restaurant; when I want amusement, I go to the theater or the concert hall; when I am sick, I go to a hospital. All we really need is a garage with a bedroom attached." But she needed something else, as modern humanity at loose ends soon finds, in a vague unhappy way.

What can the Church do? Well, we can emphasize again the timeless values which inhere in the deep relationships of life. The old-fashioned custom of having family prayers cannot always be carried through after the pattern of an earlier day, but there are many homes which are finding that a prayer at the breakfast table, a page from the "Upper Room" or some other devotional book, gives a glow to the morning which abides throughout the day.

The Bible must still ·have an honored place in the Christian home. The Church School still has parents and children alike entered upon its rolls. The Kingdom of Heaven, toward which all teaching is bent, is made up neither of slaves nor of "citizens" alien to each other, but of the sons and daughters of God. It is a filial kingdom--that is, a kingdom of sons, with God not as king but as Father. Christ is the Elder Brother, love is the law, and "peace . . . which passeth all understanding" is at the heart of all of it.

It is with this in mind that we have set apart October as "Family Month" at First Methodist Church, Fresno. Our whole Church School has come to a new day, with attendance growing every Sunday, with classes for every age. Our youth program under our new Minister of Youth is finally "on the way." And to stimulate our thinking, the worship services both morning and evening during the month will be built around the family and its problems.

In the mornings I shall preach a series, beginning October 8, on "The Dangers of Adulthood." Our evening series, with three outstanding authorities as guest· speakers, will be built around the subject "Is My Boy, Is My Girl, safe?" Then our Wednesday night "School of Religion" will make real the Old Testament for every one of us. We have a great program for the month--and I ask your support not only in attending yourselves but in bringing others with you.

Sincerely yours,[11]

~ ~ ~

Dear Friend:

We're Being Talked About!

Yes sir, you and I--and everybody else in the First Presbyterian Church of Plainville--are being talked about. Quick on the draw in criticism or praise, that's the spirit of most people toward the churches of their community.

So it's not by chance that a minister of another church told me the other day, "Your Family Night program is the best I have ever known." Or that a visitor from out of town said recently, "You folks at the First Presbyterian are envied for your Wednesday night programs." And recently a minister in another part of the state wrote, "Everybody's talking about your Family Night program. Please send me the details."

They say the things we like to have said about our Church and our program--its effectiveness, its uniqueness, its success. And they say them more convincingly than we could because, you see, its the other fellow doing the talking.

It must be remembered that our success cannot be claimed by one person or one group of persons. It came because everyone pitched in and co-operated in every way.

When the Family Night program idea was suggested two years ago, several questions arose. Would everyone join

[11] Theodore Henry Palmquist, pastor First Methodist Church, Fresno, Calif.

in the project? Could the program committee plan interesting numbers for each gathering? Would attendance hold up? Well, you know the answers. Interest grew. Attendance increased. Once more, you fine folks proved what could be done.

Now, listen: Next Wednesday night, April 25, Dr. Fred Veloz, who has spent several summers with the Indians of New Mexico, will show colored movies of his trips. In addition, a group of Indian students from King University will present several songs and dances. You'll agree that the program is one of the most informative and entertaining of the series.

So won't you take a minute right now and telephone Miss Caylor for reservations. We feel certain that you will enjoy this unique program. Wampum necessary: 65 cents a plate. Telephone 865 TODAY!

Sincerely yours,

~ ~ ~

My dear Friends:

Aren't you glad to be affiliated with a church which is truly an active church? I am thrilled to think that I am pastor of such a church! The enclosed program tells all about our activities for the six weeks ahead, until conference convenes on October 8. I hope you will read this folder and then plan to attend each of these special services.

There is a hum of activity in the air! I look from my study window and I can see the young people on their way to enroll in school for another term. I passed by the park and saw preparations being made for the homecoming. The summer is over! Fall is here! It is the time of starting again. Vacations are over and in every phase of life we are settling down to a busy schedule.

137

There begins next Sunday a very active schedule for our beloved Church. While we are having "back to school" and "back to work" activities this week, I hope you will remember that we are having "BACK TO CHURCH" SUNDAY this coming Sunday. I especially hope that you who haven't been in our church service for some time will join us this Sunday in these great services.

In days like these we need to strengthen all possible defenses. Have you found a substitute for church attendance as a means of strengthening your spiritual defenses? If so, won't you tell me about it? I have as yet discovered no substitute for church attendance! Begin Sunday to share with us in this effort to prepare ourselves to face life today. "The Ascending Life" is the title of the sermon.

The little program enclosed tells of the detailed activities, but I want to call special attention to our "Teachers' Welcome Night" for Sunday. The teachers are to be our special guests and I hope that the entire membership will be in church to welcome them. After a short service, there will be a reception with refreshments in the basement.

I hope you will accept this as a personal invitation to share in these services. Most of you I have met in these past two months. Mrs. Rupert and I have called on many of you, and we shall get around to the rest before conference. I do hope that I shall see you in church Sunday. Won't you make a special effort to be there?

I am here to serve you, and I welcome suggestions for rendering better service. I covet your advice--please share it with me. Working together, we can make our Church the vital power it should be in our community. "See you in church."

Yours in God's service,[12]

[12] Hoover Rupert, pastor of the Methodist church, Thayer, Kan.

RE-ENLISTMENT DAY NEXT SUNDAY

Dear Friend:

Vacation weeks have faded into the never-returning past, and everyone is looking forward to another year. There's increased activity everywhere in our city--the annual "hustle and bustle" to get everything in readiness for the thousands of students who will come to Norman this week for another school year.

Your Church, too, is looking forward with keen anticipation to another year of service in meeting the opportunities and fulfilling the obligations which are ours. Already, plans for many weeks ahead have been formulated by the leaders of the Church. You will be hearing about them at various times and in various ways, but today we want to tell you about the opening service of our fall program on next Sunday, September 17--RE-ENLISTMENT DAY!

This is not a financial drive, but a day when we hope to re-enlist our entire membership in the program of the Church. A special worship service has been worked out; Dr. Evans will preach a special sermon at the morning hour and Mr. Cockerill at the evening hour; Mr. Larson and his choir will be back in the choir loft; hundreds of students and visitors will be in the congregation! But unless YOU--a member of the Church--are present, it will not be a complete success.

So this letter is sent to invite you and to urge you and your family to attend RE-ENLISTMENT DAY services next Sunday. It will thrill you, as it thrills all of us, to see our great sanctuary filled to capacity, to hear hundreds of voices singing praise to our Heavenly Father, to raise with them our prayers of thanksgiving to God for his many blessings and mercies, and to enjoy fellowship with our friends and neighbors in worship.

Yes, it will be a great day--and we want YOU and YOUR FAMILY to be there and enjoy it and partake of its benefits. The services will not be complete without you, and you will be strengthened for trying days ahead by your participation in them.

Your pastors,[13]

[13] A. Norman Evans, pastor, and Herbert B. Cockerill, associate, McFarlin Memorial Methodist Church, Norman, Okla.

To inactive members

Dear Mr. and Mrs. Farley:

If you lost a diamond, you'd hunt and hunt and HUNT for it, wouldn't you?

So would we here at Central Presbyterian Church. And we <u>are</u> seeking something that is mighty valuable to <u>us</u>--your regular attendance at the midweek services.

Attendance last month was almost twice as large as in the same month last year. Ask those who attend regularly and you'll see how enthusiastic they are about the meetings. Come next Wednesday night! See how much you've been missing!

Cordially yours,

~　~　~

Dear Mr. Blake:

I wonder what has become of Joe!

Haven't you often asked yourself that same question? It might not have been "Joe," of course. Maybe his name was "Bill" or "Jim"--someone you used to know whom you have not seen for a long time, and you find yourself wondering where he is and how he is getting along.

That thought came to me this morning as I was going over our church roll. I came to your name, and immediately wondered how you were getting along.

So I am hoping that I'll see you at church next Sunday because we have missed you. I am looking forward to seeing you Sunday morning.

Cordially yours,

Dear Mrs. Maslin:

We have been missing you at church.

We need so much the encouragement of your regular presence!

Whatever the effort, come next Sunday, and regularly thereafter, won't you?

Our highest duty is the worship of God; our highest responsibility the service of Christ.

You have no idea how happy it will make us to see you this Sunday. Until then--

Sincerely yours,[14]

Move up front

Dear Friend:

Maybe you've heard the story about the hillbilly who was hunting squirrels and suddenly saw one just across the creek. Rather than take a shot from where he stood he started to walk across the stream. His companion asked, "Zeke, why don't you shoot from over here?" and he replied, "I don't want to strain my rifle."

You know, I always think of that story when I look out over the congregation and see how most of the members sit in the middle and back sections of the sanctuary. Ushers tell me that you really have to come early to get the back seats!

Really, I'm not afraid of straining myself in throwing my voice across the empty pews back to where most of you sit. It's just that I like to see you sitting just in front of me--it's an inspiring sight!

[14] Everett W. Palmer, pastor Centenary Tabernacle Methodist Church, Camden, N. J.

Won't you surprise me in the Sundays to come by taking a seat down front? As someone has said, "Many people find the church cold because they insist on sitting in 'Z' row." Come forward next Sunday!

Sincerely yours,

These are a few examples of letters which strengthen loyalty toward the church and its activites, ideals, and objectives. You will find others in Chapter 14. Some of them are personal messages, while others are directed to large groups. When planning a letter for a wide audience, write to one person—never to your mailing list. Give your letter a tone of genuineness, sincerity, and vitality. Mean what you say, and your loyalty letters will become powerful allies in your ministry.

CHAPTER 12

When It's Person to Person

WHEN an alert pastor—let's call him Mr. Mott—said to me not long ago, "I just don't have the time to keep up with my personal correspondence," I looked at him in astonishment. And yet I knew exactly what he meant.

Like scores of others, he is busy with the thousand and one duties of his pastorate. By the time he performs the role of executive, diplomat, psychologist, director of finance, teacher, minister, and many others—well, there just aren't enough hours in the day. Like his colleagues, he is compelled to work overtime in answering the many requests which come to him.

Each pastor must decide, of course, what portion of his time and facilities is to be given to a letter writing program. Of the hundreds of churches, few are without some sort of letter program. But it is safe to say that few pastors fully capitalize on the possibilities of building good will through their personal correspondence. The limited number who have demonstrated the tremendous pulling power of effective letters in "making friends and influencing people" can point to results, both tangible and intangible.

When all the evidence is collected and weighed, two sound conclusions become apparent: (1) Personal letters can be a powerful factor in improving public relations of pastor and church. (2) Few pastors have even begun to utilize the potentialities of this aid to their ministries.

Letter writing pays

And just how do these conclusions apply to you and your church? That's easy. Make the most of every contact in your personal letters. These messages will show returns immeasurably greater than the small time required to write them. Put them to work for you!

On many occasions, your "good intentions" suggest a letter. But don't just intend to write or answer a message. Do it! Whatever the circumstances, be natural, sincere, and human. Say what is in your heart, and your letter will be an accurate reflection of YOU.

Letters of acknowledgment, birthday greetings, notes required by your professional relationships, congratulatory messages, "thank you" letters, courtesy notes, expressions of sympathy—these and countless others provide opportunities for you to show others that you are thoughtful, gracious, and prompt in your friendly relations.

Really, there's no limit to the uses of the personal letter in strengthening friendships with others. Thanks for gifts must be written. A letter telling a minister elsewhere of a new procedure you are finding effective may be of real value to him, and it will certainly make him wish to reciprocate when an opportunity arises. "Thank you" notes for hospitality are a "must." A message congratulating an elderly pastor on his birthday and thanking him for his counsel to you in your early days in the ministry will give him a new joy. Frequently you will write a sincere message of sympathy to those who are grieved or disappointed. And you must acknowledge letters from members of other churches which you have served. These and numerous other situations offer opportunities for you to build your personal public relations by means of friendly notes. Here are a number of effective examples.

Speaking engagements

Dear Mr. Douglass:

It will be a real pleasure for me to address members of the Tulsa Young Men's Christian Association at their annual banquet at Hotel Warren Tuesday evening, June 4, at seven o'clock.

My subject will be "Priorities in Personality." Soon I shall send a brief biographical sketch and also the newspaper mat which you requested.

On every hand I have heard many fine compliments regarding your work as secretary, and I am sure that much of the progress of the "Y" is due to your splendid leadership.

Cordially yours,

~ ~ ~

Dear Miss Sargent:

I just want to tell you what a pleasure it was to be with you and your group Tuesday afternoon, and to thank you for accepting me in the role of substitute.

Nothing is contributing quite as much to the youth program in our community as your committee. Through your splendid work, our teen-agers will have wholesome recreation instead of "wreckreation."

Please let me know whenever I can be of help.

Sincerely yours,

145

Dear Mr. Meacham:

It is very complimentary of you to believe that the address I made at the recent assembly at Municipal University would interest the readers of your monthly magazine, the "Campus Reflector."

Enclosed is a copy of the address, which you may want to shorten somewhat to meet your space requirements. Also, you will find the glossy photograph which you requested.

It was a delightful pleasure to visit your splendid institution and to meet so many faculty members and students.

Please send me two copies of the magazine when it comes from the press.

Sincerely yours,

~ ~ ~

Dear Mr. Washington:

Thank you for your kind letter in which you invite me to speak at the October 12 meeting of the Bryan County School Administrators' Association. Naturally, I am delighted to come.

Acting on your suggestion, I shall include a few comments on ways of improving church-school relationships. My subject will be "The Teaching Function of the Church."

Later on, please inform me of the time and place of the meeting.

Never was there a time when the profession of education carried such a heavy responsibility, never a time when its members might feel a greater pride in the significance of their work. You and your fellow administrators are doing a magnificent work in the face of unusual difficulties.

Cordially yours,

Dear Jim:

Thank you so much for sending me a copy of the Middletown "Daily Banner" which carried a story regarding my address at the recent meeting of your ministerial alliance.

It was a delightful pleasure to visit with you again and to meet other pastors of your city. Several have been gracious enough to write expressing their appreciation for my address.

I hope to see you again soon.

Cordially yours,

~ ~ ~

Dear Mr. Drake:

Nothing would please me more than to participate in the panel discussion on "Religion in the Postwar World" to be given at the Y. M. C. A. in Montrose, Wednesday night, April 4.

But much to my regret, your meeting comes at a time when I shall be conducting pre-Easter services at the First Baptist Church in Decatur.

Your program is most timely and is certain to be enjoyable and profitable for all who attend.

Thank you for thinking of me, and do let me know if I can be of assistance in the future.

Sincerely yours,

Acknowledging gifts

Dear Mr. Blain:

How nice of you to give me a subscription to my favorite magazine, "Pulpit Digest." Twelve gifts instead of one!

It's just like you to think of something so much desired. Truly you have been so generous and thoughtful that I am pressed for new ways to thank you. But I do sincerely appreciate all you have done.

Sincerely yours,

~ ~ ~

Dear Mr. and Mrs. May:

It was very fine of you to continue to remember me by sending me for Christmas the book "Take a Look at Yourself," by John Homer Miller.

You may be surprised to learn that I read it in two nights. Readable and provocative, it gave me much enjoyment and will be of great value to me in my ministry. Thank you so much.

Best wishes to both of you for the New Year.

Cordially yours,

Dear Mrs. Rushing:

Mrs. Mosely and I are most grateful to members of the Ladies' Aid for giving us the beautiful lamp at the recent farewell reception in our honor.

To us it will always typify the rare illumination, the Christ-like light, which characterizes the membership and activities of the Ladies' Aid of Kenton City. Please express our appreciation to members of the organization and tell them that we shall always treasure it along with their friendship and love.

Cordially and faithfully,

Higdon Mosely

148

"Thank you" letters

Dear Mr. and Mrs. Ray:

It was a delight to have the privilege of being in your home and of renewing my friendship with both of you last week.

How proud you must be of Bob. It is most remarkable that he is a member of the high school debate team although he is just a freshman. His future is bright.

If you are ever in this section of the state, please remember that we shall expect you to stop over with us.

Sincerely yours,

~ ~ ~

Dear Mrs. Kirk:

Was there ever such a happy dinner party as yours last night! The food was perfection, of course, and your guests were delightful persons. It was most interesting to hear Captain Kelchner tell of his experiences in India.

It was so kind of you to share your brilliant friends and your beautiful house with Mrs. Evans and me. We had a wonderful time--the best ever. Thank you for a lovely evening.

Sincerely yours,

Wesley Evans

Dear Arnold:

It was a thrill for all of us to hear you sing "The Holy City" at our Palm Sunday services. Through the years I have heard the number many times, including presentations by nationally known artists, but never before have I heard it interpreted with such feeling as you put into it. My, but it stirred our souls!

I was terribly sorry that because of the funeral services I couldn't visit with you longer before you went to the bus station. But maybe we can get together when I come to Middleberg for a pastors' conference early in May.

Thank you again for giving us the gospel in song. It will long be remembered by all of us.

Cordially yours,

~ ~ ~

Dear Mr. and Mrs. Mennen:

After such a charming week end in your home, Mrs. Palmer and I find ourselves still living over certain moments and delights. We came home refreshed in mind and with energy enough to make the week hum.

Thank you for inviting us and for giving us such a happy time.

Cordially yours,

Frank Palmer

150

Dear Mr. Beaty:

Thank you so much for inviting me to attend the recent assembly which was held at Longfellow High School as the first event of your annual Religious Emphasis Week.

Congratulations to you, and to your teachers and students, for originating and conducting such a splendid program. It is certain to make a tremendous impact in developing the leaders of tomorrow.

Through your excellent work our young people's program, as well as those in other churches, has grown in interest.

We thank you sincerely for your wholehearted co-operation.

Cordially yours,

Professional relationships

Dear Mr. Riggs:

Today's issue of the Detroit "News" brought the joyous story that you and your congregation will dedicate your new church next Sunday.

Sincere congratulations to you and your members in completing this beautiful structure. With more than usual interest, I looked at the pictures and read the description of the many and varied facilities of your church.

I am sure that this achievement is due largely to your vision, your executive ability, your notable Christian leadership, and your remarkable talent for doing everything well.

At the earliest opportunity I want to visit your new church.

Very best wishes for the summer.

Yours sincerely,

151

Dear Mr. Hopper:

You really hit the nail on the head in your excellent article "Making Assistant Pastors Out of Laymen," which I have just read in the current issue of the "Church Digest."

Your splendid suggestions are valuable to all ministers, and I shall use many of them in my program here. I was especially interested in your comments regarding new tasks for laymen.

Your article came to my attention at a time when I was puzzled as to the most effective ways of training workers. But now that I have your welcome advice, I am going to train at least fifty people capable of the finest type of evangelistic work. And one of these days soon, when we begin to see results, you'll know that you had a great part in our success.

Sincerely yours,

~ ~ ~

Dear Bishop Barnes:

On the occasion of your sixtieth birthday, I want to send you this brief message of congratulation and my sincere wish that you may enjoy the best of health for years to come.

You know that we are all proud of you--for all that you are and for all that you have done.

I hope that your sixtieth milestone will be a happy day, and that the Lord will continue to bless you in doing his will.

Cordially yours,

~ ~ ~

Dear Dr. McKee:

I was mighty glad to hear that your people gave you a surprise dinner to commemorate your fifteen years as pastor of the First Methodist Church. What a fine tribute to you for your many years of service in advancing the Kingdom!

You can take great pride in the thousands of lives which you have lifted and ennobled. Through your ministry they have been fed the bread of life. Both by precept and example, you ·have given others an increased loyalty to Christ and his Church.

This letter brings best wishes and my profound gratitude to you for giving the highest possible service to Christ's cause.

Sincerely yours,

~   ~   ~

Dear Bert:

Because of a speaking engagement here, I had to leave the Kansas City pastors' meeting a day before it closed. So I did not have a chance to tell you how much I enjoyed your excellent paper on church finance.

You made a real contribution to the program and I, for one, shall soon put several of your fine ideas into practice here.

It was good to see you again, though I wish we might have had a longer visit between sessions. Perhaps we can get together and have another visit for a while at the state meeting in Joplin.

Cordially yours,

~   ~   ~

Dear Oscar:

You certainly made a hit! Members of my congregation enjoyed your two sermons so much, in fact, that we want to have you with us again soon.

I want to assure you of my grateful appreciation for your services. Enclosed is a check which expresses in a small way our thanks to you.

Elizabeth and I enjoyed our vacation in the mountains. The fish must have been on their vacation, too, because I didn't get a strike! But we did enjoy a wonderful rest because we led a lazy existence.

Thanks again for everything.

Cordially yours,

~ ~ ~

Dear Bob:

Here's good news for you. Mrs. Bernice Kimball, who will soon transfer her membership from my Church to yours, is one of the most devoted and enthusiastic workers I have ever known.

Her activities here were so many and varied that it is impossible to enumerate them all. Although she has done outstanding work in several phases of our program, to me, her real achievements lie in her remarkable ability to direct the work of students of high school age.

As you know, a person must possess a certain "plus" in personality to attract and hold young people. Mrs. Kimball possesses this rare quality, as you will discover when you give her an assignment.

Her leaving is a real loss to us, but I am delighted that she will be associated with you in Springfield.

Be sure to drop in for a visit next time you are in Valley City.

Sincerely yours,

Dear Mr. Gaston:

Welcome to Brownwood! I am sure you will enjoy your ministry at the First Christian Church, and that you will like Brownwood--everybody does.

In all my years as a minister, I have never served in a community where there is such a fine spirit of co-operation as I have found here. Church leaders and laymen alike work together in harmony and in love.

You are cordially invited to attend the next meeting of the Brownwood Ministerial Alliance, which will be held in the pastor's study at the First Presbyterian Church, Main at Akard, Tuesday afternoon, April 17, at 2:30. I am looking forward to meeting you at that time.

Cordially yours,

~ ~ ~

Dear Mr. Greever:

It is a pleasure to recommend Miss Elizabeth Rohrer for a position as secretary in the office of the Middletown Council of Churches.

During her two years as one of the secretaries in our Church her work was more than satisfactory--it was excellent. She is an expert stenographer and is accurate in all phases of her work. Miss Rohrer is alert, resourceful, and highly intelligent. Added to these attributes, her pleasant personality and willingness to co-operate make her unusually successful in working with others.

I recommend this young woman to you without reservation, for I am confident that she will prove a very satisfactory staff member.

Yours very truly,

155

Dear Mr. Farley:

I was ever so sorry to learn from last night's "Tribune" of the water damage to the basement of your church following the heavy rains Tuesday and Wednesday.

Although few details were given in the news story, I sincerely hope that the damage to furniture and other equipment proves to be less than you expect.

If there is anything we at the Belleview Baptist can do to help, please call on us.

Sincerely yours,

~ ~ ~

Dear Mervin:

This letter will be handed you by my friend and associate Theodore Hyde, one of the outstanding leaders of my Church.

Mr. Hyde has heard of your excellent training program for church ushers, and he is anxious to develop a similar one here. If it is convenient for you to explain your program to him I shall appreciate it, and I know you will have his gratitude for any courtesy you may show him.

Very sincerely yours,

~ ~ ~

Dear Booker:

It was a disappointment to learn from your letter of April 7 that you will not be with us at the religious education conference in Wichita next week.

Since I know you had looked forward to Bishop Oxnam's two lectures, I shall jot down a few notes and send you a typed copy upon my return.

We shall all miss you, but here's hoping that you can attend the fall meeting in Topeka.

Cordially,

~ ~ ~

Dear Clyde:

I have just learned of your resignation from the executive board of the Methodist Orphans' Home.

This has been a "labor of love," and I doubt that any person has contributed more to the progress of the home than you have. May you always be happy in the thought that you have left behind a record of loyalty and devotion.

Congratulations on your outstanding record of service, and best wishes for the many years ahead.

Sincerely,

~ ~ ~

Dear Crawford:

Arthur Christy told me last night that you will soon be leaving your present pastorate to become professor of religion at Midwest Theological Seminary.

Personally, my only regret is that your new position will take you out of this conference. You will be doing an important work, however, and I know you will deeply influence the hundreds of students who will be in your classes.

By every standard of measurement you have earned this honor, and I am delighted that it has come to you. Congratulations to you and congratulations to the college.

Cordially,

~ ~ ~

Dear Mr. Geist:

Yesterday afternoon I read your excellent article in the October issue of the "Pastor." You have presented the soundest treatment of church advertising that I've ever seen.

Congratulations on this fine article. All of us who are interested in new techniques of layouts will profit from your splendid contribution.

Sincerely yours,

Acknowledging letters of thanks

Dear Josephine:

Your letter of March 25 gave me a lot of pleasure. Thank you for your thoughtfulness in writing it.

From time to time I hear of your achievements at Clark University. I congratulate you upon your fine record and wish you every success in maintaining it during the years ahead.

Although we miss you greatly in our young people's activities, we are delighted that your talent has already been discovered by Wesley Foundation leaders in Scranton.

Thank you again for your letter of appreciation. I shall be happy to see you when you come home for the holidays.

Cordially yours,

Dear Mr. Mahier:

Thank you, sincerely, for your very nice note. It was a great pleasure for me to serve as one of the judges at the annual Boy Scout hobby show.

All of these pessimists who keep insisting that today's youth are on the wrong track would certainly change their minds if they could see how you and your associates are promoting such a worth-while program of activities.

If I may be of service to you on future occasions, please call on me.

Sincerely yours,

~ ~ ~

Dear Mr. Bealer:

Your gracious letter of thanks regarding the recent district laymen's banquet in our church is appreciated very much. Such a message means a great deal to me, for we did work hard on the arrangements.

Most of the credit should go to the officers of our group, who worked for several months on preliminary details.

Thank you again for your letter, and remember that you are always welcome at the First Presbyterian.

Cordially yours,

~ ~ ~

Dear Mrs. Hatton:

Your generous compliment upon last week's "Chapel of the Air" broadcasts is much appreciated. Thoughtful letters like yours certainly add zest to my work.

Mr. Lloyd DeWeese, program director for the radio station, asked that I appear again on the series for the week of March 5 to 9, and I hope that you will be a regular listener each morning. Your comments will be most welcome.

Thank you again for such high praise.

Cordially yours,

Acknowledging congratulatory notes

Dear Mr. Little:

Thank you for your gracious note. Of course, I was quite happy to be elected president of the Parkersburg Ministerial Alliance, because I consider it a high honor.

Never, in all my ministry, have I found such devoted and enthusiastic pastors as we have in this city. It will be a real joy to work with them in uplifting the religious life of our citizens.

But as you realize, the ultimate success of our activities and objectives will depend to a great extent on the loyalty and co-operation of leading laymen like you. Indeed, our dreams would come true if we could develop in all people the love which you hold for your Church.

Thank you again for your thoughtfulness in writing.

Sincerely,

~ ~ ~

Dear Larry:

No one could have appreciated that thoughtful note of yours more than I did. To be quite truthful, my election as chairman of the Burlington Council of Churches came as a real surprise to me, and, of course, I was flattered by the honor.

160

I have watched your progress with great interest, and I am very happy that I came to know you and that I have been able in any small way to help you.

Because of your interest in our Church and its activities, I shall send you copies of our monthly newspaper in the future.

Very best wishes to you.

Sincerely yours,

Declining invitations

Dear Mr. Logan:

Thank you so much for your invitation to attend Dr. Richard Ivester's lecture on "The Changing Indian" at the Men's Dinner Club April 25. Dr. Ivester's magazine articles always interest me, and for that reason I would like to hear him.

But upon checking my calendar, I discover that I must attend a special meeting of ministers in Jacksonville that night.

I am extremely sorry that it will be impossible for me to be present at your meeting and also enjoy a visit with you.

Thank you again for your thoughtfulness.

Sincerely yours,

~ ~ ~

Dear Edson:

Your letter extending me so cordial an invitation to be the guest of the Cedarvale Chamber of Commerce at the tenth annual banquet January 21 is deeply appreciated.

Nothing would give me greater pleasure, but it happens that I shall be in Dallas at a meeting of the Conference Board on Missions at that time.

161

You have done so much for the organization that I feel that our entire citizenship owes a great debt of gratitude to you.

Do drop in for a visit the next time you are in Ardmore.

Sincerely yours,

Miscellaneous letters

Dear Mr. Eckhart:

Thank you for your letter of October 20.

I shall be delighted to serve on the citizens committee of the Stidger Memorial Library during 194--.

I feel that it is an honor to become a member of your group, and I shall make every effort to fulfill the responsibilities which membership entails.

Sincerely yours,

~ ~ ~

Dear Mr. Shorter:

Your cordial invitation for me to join the National Church Newswriters' Association pleases me very much, and I accept with pleasure.

I consider it a privilege to join such an outstanding group of religious leaders and writers, and I welcome the opportunity to participate in your activities.

Please express my sincere thanks to other members of the membership committee.

Cordially yours,

162

Dear Mr. Lenox:

You will never know how disappointed I was to learn, upon returning to Quincy this week, that I had missed you when you called by to see me. As my secretary probably told you, I was in Kansas City at a conference for recreation leaders.

It was nice of you to stop to see me, and I am hoping that your work will bring you back this way soon. In fact, let me know when you are coming through the Middle West and we'll get together for our long-overdue visit.

Cordially yours,

From these examples, you can see the untold possibilities in friendly, personalized messages. By using them, you can keep your friendships in good repair, increase professional prestige, create good will in minor contacts, and elevate your standing as a minister by expanding the areas of your influence. By all means, then, give your personal correspondence a "top-drawer" position in your letter schedule, and the results will be amazing. Try it and see!

Capitalizing on Civic Contacts

IF THE many and varied services of the modern church are to be successful, they must first be assured of a happy reception by the community of which they are a part. . . . And interestingly enough, what [the] public thinks of you and your church—rather than what you think of it—gauges the success or failure of your enterprise."[1]

By maintaining a harmonious relationship with community leaders—those who are vital in creating public opinion in your city—you can strengthen the collective opinion regarding you and your church.

How often have you resolved to write a brief note of thanks to the newspaper editor for publishing so much church news? Did you ever express your appreciation to the chief of police for providing an escort for funeral processions? You heard that the Lions Club was providing free tonsillectomies for underprivileged children, but did you ever write a note of thanks to the president? Think of the many other public-spirited citizens who are helping you in making your city a better place in which to live.

You and your community

As a minister, you have a goal and a vision for your people and for your community. Mark Rich once pointed out,

[1] Harral, *Public Relations for Churches* (New York and Nashville: Abingdon-Cokesbury Press, 1945), pp. 16, 18.

in the *Pulpit*: "He [the minister] has a holy dissatisfaction with some aspects of individual and community life. Thus he is always living in two worlds: the community that is and the one that is to be. . . . He is like the wise men who saw a star and followed after it. He is on his way. He not only looks forward to the coming of the Kingdom but is taking steps to bring it into fulfillment in his community."

Every force which ennobles and lifts the lives of people deserves your support. Strengthen one unit of Christianity and you strengthen them all. But even the most enthusiastic joiner cannot affiliate with each and every one of the numerous social-interest groups so characteristic of our culture. Rather, the busy pastor must participate in as many community-betterment programs as time permits, and then maintain friendly relations with leaders in other areas of civic improvement.

Community contacts are of numerous types. Frequently the pastor is a leader in various civic, cultural, character-building, and humanitarian enterprises of his city. On other occasions the general public, as well as special groups, are brought into close relationship with the church through certain programs, activities, and events.

Increasing appreciation

In addition to these contacts, a pastor can instill a genuine sense of appreciation and worth of himself and his church through friendly letters to community leaders. Congratulatory notes, letters of invitation to church events, and many other types may be used in developing a close and harmonious association between the church and "first citizens" of the community.

Here are several examples of effective letters to community leaders. Such messages, of course, should be individually typed and completely personalized.

Dear Mr. Caudill:

This morning I learned that you have been elected chairman of the Middletown Youth Commission, and this note carries my hearty congratulations upon such recognition of your ability.

You will do excellent work for our community in your new capacity, I know, for doing things well is a habit of yours in anything you undertake.

Whenever any of us at Central Baptist Church can assist you in any way, I know you will feel free to call upon us.

Sincerely yours,

~ ~ ~

Dear Mr. Anderson:

Welcome to Middletown! Hearty congratulations on being named principal of Longfellow High School.

Through the years the First Presbyterian Church has enjoyed the finest relationships with our public schools and we are anxious to co-operate with you in every possible way.

Whenever occasion permits, I shall be very glad to have you drop by to see me.

Cordially yours,

~ ~ ~

Dear Mr. Hess:

This is just a word to tell you how much all of us appreciate your splendid work as chairman of the Middletown Bible Society during the past year.

Under your leadership, the organization was engaged in a number of excellent activities. But to me the most outstanding service was the plan which you started of sending Bibles to local men and women now in the armed forces.

Sincere good wishes to you for a happy and prosperous New Year.

Cordially yours,

~ ~ ~

Dear Mr. Epton:

Congratulations to you and your deputies for your laudable work in ridding our city and county of slot machines.

All of us know that these "one-armed bandits" are dishonest and that they exist mainly for folks who believe that somehow they can win from these devices.

You are doing an exceptionally fine piece of work in abolishing these machines, and I want to congratulate you and your deputies upon taking the lead in a movement of far-reaching importance to our citizenship.

Keep up the good work!

Sincerely yours,

~ ~ ~

Dear Ben:

I was glad to see in yesterday's Blankville "Times" that you have been elected president of the Red River Valley Boy Scout Council for the coming year.

From watching your work as scoutmaster and as director of the high school group in our Church, I know that you will do a splendid job. In fact, your promotion to a post of such responsibility proves that you have been doing just that in the past.

Hearty congratulations and best wishes for your continued success.

Cordially yours,

~ ~ ~

Dear Mr. Story:

This is just a little note to tell you how much we all appreciate your paper's generous use of news concerning events and activities of the First Presbyterian Church.

Your help is appreciated more than ever today because I realize that every day you face the problem of selection from a great volume of news to use in a greatly reduced space.

You have the gratitude of officials and members, as well as my deep personal appreciation, for the loyal interest you have always shown in church activities of our city.

Cordially yours,

~ ~ ~

Dear Mr. Hargrove:

You are cordially invited to hear an address by Charles M. Hyde, expert on church finance from Boston, in the church library at eleven o'clock Tuesday morning, October 14.

I am inviting you and a few other leaders from other churches to be my special guests on this occasion, and I should like very much for you to attend.

168

After the program Mrs. Russell is planning to give us lunch, and we can enjoy a good visit at my home.

Sincerely yours,

Gordon Russell

~ ~ ~

Dear Mr. Kendall:

What's the truth about religion in Russia?

We shall have an opportunity to hear the answers to that question Tuesday night, September 5, at eight o'clock, when Dr. Harold Ward, professor of history at T--- University, speaks to us in the church parlor.

Dr. Ward, one of the outstanding laymen of our denomination, spent two years in Russia and is author of the book "Russia Faces the Future."

We feel most fortunate in being able to bring this eminent historian and churchman to Middletown, and we hope that you can be with us for his appearance here.

Sincerely yours,

~ ~ ~

Dear Homer:

Last night's GAZETTE brought the good news that you have been elected president of the Middletown Rotary Club for the coming year.

With your genuine interest in civic betterment and your ability to do everything to perfection, I'm sure that the club will make great progress under your leadership.

Heartiest congratulations! I'll see you one of these days, but I felt that this couldn't wait.

Sincerely yours,

Granting that you have a crowded schedule, allow time to write more friendly letters to "key" individuals of your city. Even if it were possible, you never want your church as a social institution to be hung in space and insulated from all contacts with community life. You want its full impact to be felt by those who "cross the crowded ways of life." Join with others who are improving the spiritual climate of your community and, at the same time, use letters to cement harmonious relationships. Put these good-will builders to work for you!

CHAPTER 14

Tested Letters That Click

NOW that we have considered the vital do's and don'ts of church letters and have seen a number of specimen examples, let's examine some tested letters that have been successfully used by pastors. Few of the letters are perfect —indeed, most of their authors will agree that the messages could be improved.

The fifty-five letters that appear on the following pages deal with a wide variety of church situations. They include attendance letters, birthday greetings, Thanksgiving messages, Sunday school letters, notes of appreciation, and letters for many other occasions. Obviously, there is some difference in their quality, but interestingly enough, each one performed its mission.

As you evaluate these specimens you will naturally be watching for the numerous faults and virtues discussed and illustrated in preceding chapters. But instead of being too critical, ask yourself after reading each one, "Could I have done as well?" Perhaps the most interesting test will be for you to determine precisely how YOU would react to each letter if it had been sent to you. After all, that's the most human test and the most reliable.

Finally, the following letters show a wide variety of approaches to a church's public relations problems. But all of them have one very important element in common—they got results! Each one proved its effectiveness by building good will, co-operation, or support; and equally important, each one extended the ministry of its church.

Acknowledging gifts

Dear Mr. Simonds:

Thank you so much for your gift to our Chimes Fund.

This morning I received a letter from the factory stating that the chimes will be installed during the latter part of the month. So it won't be long until we hear them ring out over our city. And when they do they will make for a very real spiritual extention of our Church.

Not far in the future the magic of heavenly music, coming from the chimes of our Church, will impart spiritual strength to thousands in our community. And when that occurs you will know that you had a part in its realization.

Cordially yours,

~ ~ ~

Dear Mrs. Bronson:

Mrs. J. H. Smith, superintendent of our High School Department, told me today of your gift of the beautiful picture "The Last Supper" to that department.

We appreciate ever so much this act of thoughtfulness on your part, and of course we are delighted to receive this lovely picture. It will be an inspiration to all who see it.

Thank you again for your gift, and for the Christian spirit which prompted it.

Sincerely yours,

172

Dear Mrs. Rowe:

Thank you for your kindness in presenting several of your books to the Wesley Foundation.

In a count made Monday we discovered that almost four hundred books have been given by members of our Church. As soon as they are catalogued and new shelves are constructed we would like so much for you to visit our library.

We of the Foundation--every one of us--deeply appreciate your co-operation in this venture. We shall always be grateful to you because you helped us to make one of our dreams come true.

Sincerely yours,

Director

Anniversary

Dear Friend:

You weren't there. All of us weren't there. But something splendid, magnificent happened in 1862. THEY, the founders, began our great Church.

It cradled our new-born spirits, nurtured our growth as Christians, stirred our consciences, washed away our fears. It has been a pillar of strength and a light of goodness in the community.

Millions of individual worship experiences have carried the Christian message from the sanctuary into life's proving ground. Millions of hours of unheralded service have been given my humble Christians, an offering to Oakland and the wider world.

You loved the music. You were quickened by the preaching. You loved one of the ministers, or perhaps several of them.

You infused your life into the boys and girls of a Sunday School class--or you were one of the restless crew. You were the Church and the Church was you.

Now we want you to come and help us celebrate this EIGHTIETH ANNIVERSARY on Sunday, October 25, between 9:45 A. M. and 4:30 P. M. See our renewal of part of the "new" church. Renew "auld acquaintance." Draw again some of the old-time spirit for your new-time needs.

We enclose a HERALD which tells more about it, and provides a coupon to mail. (Or send a postal.) Won't you send it now?

We anticipate the pleasure of your presence. Your sacrifice of time, effort, and expense will reward you richly, and bless us all. If circumstances positively forbid, will you write us a greeting. Send or lend us a bit of memory material you may have, or in some other manner have a share.

Fraternally,

Minister

Chairman of Celebration Committee [1]

Appreciation

Dear Mr. Smith:

Your period of active service as an officer of First Presbyterian Church has come to a close, at least temporarily, as you know. I cannot let the occasion pass without expressing to you my sincere personal thanks for your co-operation as a lay leader in the Church.

[1] Used by Frank Morey Toothaker, pastor First Methodist Church, Oakland, Calif.

174

To that I would also add the thanks of the congregation which elected you to office and which you have served so faithfully. The whole Church is greatly in your debt. After the necessary waiting period is ended, I hope that you may serve actively again. In the meantime, I know that you will continue to support the Church and lead it forward in service to God's Kingdom.

In case you had not thought about it, let me remind you that as an ordained officer of the Church you are eligible to hold the same position in any Presbyterian Church in the country without being ordained again. Once you are ordained to a church office the ordination is permanent, even though you may at times be on the inactive list.

With warmest personal greetings,[2]

Attendance

Dear Friends of Eastern Avenue Church:

Some time ago, in the "American Magazine," an article appeared entitled "Why I Don't Go to Church." Thousands of people took up the challenge of the author. The best reply came from a college student. His letter is so fine and expresses my own feelings so well that I want to share it with you. Here it is:

"We who are just growing into maturity are seeking something in the Church which we cannot find elsewhere--understanding through Jesus Christ, understanding of ideals through which we and all about us can live happier, better lives.

"I am a senior at the University of Minnesota, a fraternity man interested in campus activities, and earn my way through school as business manager of the world's largest college newspaper. I attend convocations and student forums, participate in intramural sports, and take part in a weekly student broadcast.

"I enjoy a game of golf, a rubber of bridge, an intelligent moving picture, and wish that I could find more time for these

[2] Harry Bertrand Taylor, pastor First Presbyterian Church, Syracuse, N. Y.

THE FOURTH PRESBYTERIAN CHURCH

Dr. Alexis Carrel, a physician, a scientist, and the co-inventor, with Charles A. Lindbergh, of the mechanical heart, recently told a patient:

"Go to church. You'll feel better."

And Dr. Carrel is not the only scientist who knows that churchgoing really works. Psychologists, whose lifework is devoted to examining the minds of men, agree that individuals who attend a church get along better with themselves and with others than those who do not.

There's a reason for that—and Dr. Carrel has put it into words as well as anyone I have ever heard.

You do feel better when you go to church.

You have a sense of belonging—belonging to a great group of people devoted to a common cause.

You gain a feeling of restfulness—the sense of peace that comes from a quiet period of meditation undisturbed by worldly affairs.

You get a feeling of security—the knowledge that there is one institution that has withstood the buffets of 1900 years of storm and strife.

And all these add up to a sense of strength—the strength to carry on throughout the week with the inspiration given to you by a Sunday morning at church.

Come to church next Sunday. You'll feel better. May I look for you then?

Sincerely,

Charles Eaton

Minister

Used by permission of A. B. Dick Company, Chicago, Ill.

recreations. Often there are so many things to do, so many projects to be completed, that I don't know what to do next. Still, I take time to go to church.

"Sunday comes. I sit in church listening to the soft tremolo of the organ and the matched voices of the choir. The pastor gives a sermon on the life of Christ. I feel like a different person; a powerful sense of well-being comes over me. A better understanding of Christ orients me for the coming week; I am ready to start work again.

"It is not the exhortations of the evangelist which move me. He, to me, is a dealer in emotions transitory at best, and his plea to come forward leaves me unaffected. It is, mystical though it may sound, a sort of 'communion with God' in a quiet, thoughtful atmosphere that touches a responsive chord in me and moves me to strive for a more pure life.

"It is this understanding of life through the teachings of Jesus that I find so stimulating in religion. I need this understanding, this stabilizing influence, this help in solving problems beyond the psychiatrist's realm, and so I go to church."

I sincerely hope that Eastern Avenue Church can give as much to you.

Faithfully,[3]

Baptism

Dear Eugene:

I just wanted you to know what a thrilling experience it was to share in the baptism service for you and your father. It is a tremendously important occasion in the life of any family when a member decides to bear the mark of Christ and to be known as a follower of His in the community around him.

[3] Used by permission A. B. Dick Company, Chicago, Ill. Quoted letter, by a senior at the University of Minnesota, appeared in the *American Magazine* for February 1938. Used by permission.

I know that your father and you must have much in common in the realization that you went through this very sacred service together, and I just want to say that I hope this decision on the part of both of you to confess and to profess the Christian faith will give you the strength and joy which alone enables one to run at life triumphantly.

This letter is not only to wish you well on the adventure upon which you have embarked, but it is also to say that in the future I shall be happy to learn of anything I can do to help you achieve the ideals set up before you in the promises you made at the altar of the Church.

As the years pass, I hope the Christian faith will come to mean as much to you as it does to me, and there are no words in our English tongue to indicate all it means to me.

Cordially yours,[4]

Birth message

Dear Mary:

The word of your safe arrival in our strange world has brought much joy to the hearts of the friends of your parents. We rejoice with them over your having made such a wise choice of your parents, your neighborhood, and your country--we also want to say your Church, for it is our hope that you will grow up in your own household of faith, where many hands of fellowship and encouragement will always be stretched out to help you.

We pray God's richest blessing upon you as you begin your pilgrimage through life. Let us hope that your generation may build a world of brotherhood and peace.

I am enclosing some verses for your mother which have been written by different poets telling of the joy which a baby like you brings.

[4] Robert Leonard Tucker, pastor First Methodist Church, New Haven, Conn.

Your name has been placed on our Cradle Roll, and a year from now you will receive a birthday card from our Church School.

Sincerely yours,[5]

Birthday greetings

Happy Birthday to You!

My Christian Friend:

According to my birthday book, you will have a birthday next week.

Your pastor has been following the custom of setting aside a portion of each day for special prayer to God for the members and friends of Christ Lutheran Church. Since it is impossible to pray for sixteen hundred people by name each day, I plan to follow regularly this fall and winter a systematic, daily period of prayer for those whose birthdays come within the period of the following week, beginning with Monday and including Sunday.

Your name appears on my list for next week. I want you to know that each day between 6:30 A. M. and 7:30 A. M. I shall definitely pray for you by name. My purpose in acquainting you with this program of prayer is twofold.

First: I am confident that if you know that each day at this hour your pastor is praying for you, you will draw near to God at that same time, or at some other time of day, for prayer. Jesus says: "I say unto you, That if two of you shall agree on earth as touching any thing that they shall ask, it shall be done for them of my Father which is in heaven" (Matthew 18:19).

[5] This letter, written to each new baby of the congregation, is usually sent to the hospital a day or two after the baby's birth. With each letter are enclosed two pages of mimeographed poems. Used by Stanley Armstrong Hunter, pastor St. John's Presbyterian Church, Berkeley, Calif.

Second: To let you know that your pastor remembers your birthday. Then, too, it will open the way for you, if you wish, to call your pastor and have a heart-to-heart interview with him concerning anything that may rest heavily upon your soul. Feel free to call at the parsonage, to phone, or to write. I shall count it a privilege to be of help to you.

I also invite your daily prayers for your pastor, your Church, and for God's blessing upon every endeavor of our church program. "Bear ye one another's burdens, and so fulfill the law of Christ." (Galatians 6:2.)

Faithfully and sincerely

Your pastor,[6]

Building fund

Dear Friend of Epworth:

Attached is a ONE DOLLAR BILL which will bring you a great store of fun and entertainment if you follow the instructions below.

WHAT TO DO - Invest this dollar in some way in which it will earn at least two dollars profit. (We hope you will find some clever way in which it will earn several dollars.) Try to invest it in some unusual way for reasons you will learn later in this letter.

WHEN TO DO IT - Invest this dollar as soon as you receive it-- the sooner it is invested the more it may earn!

WHY DO IT - Epworth Church is in need of several repairs, and the official board of the Church would rather not spon-

[6] This letter, written by the Rev. J. E. Rudisill, is reprinted from *Church Business,* a publication of the Duplex Envelope Company, Richmond, Va.

sor a special campaign but intends to build up a fund to care for this need over a period of time. The Building Fund Committee is attempting to raise this fund without sponsoring a "high pressure campaign," and we believe those who have an interest in the Church will appreciate this effort. We can have some real enjoyment in accomplishing this goal, and this is one of the ways of doing it.

FOR HOW LONG - Invest your dollar NOW, and then return this dollar plus the profit at our CHURCH NITE to be held on the evening of NOVEMBER THE NINTH. (Further details will reach you by mail.)

CHURCH NITE - On Friday evening, November 9, we will enjoy a program at the church. During the course of the evening reports will be made as to the various ways in which dollars were invested and the amounts they earned. If each dollar is invested in some unusual or comical way, we should enjoy one of the most entertaining evenings in the history of our Church. The grand total will be announced at the close of the evening-- HELP MAKE IT A GRAND TOTAL!

SUGGESTIONS - Please remember to invest your dollar in some legitimate way--the Church does not sponsor raffles, bingo, etc. Find some unusual way to put your dollar to work.

One woman bought material and made and sold aprons.

One man bought a trapping license and trapped muskrats.

A man bought shampoo and washed ladies' hair, and his daughter waved the hair.

A woman (54 years old) bought Simonize and simonized cars.

Now begin thinking, for you are about to enter the business world to invest a BIG dollar for your entertainment and for the BUILD-ING FUND of Epworth Methodist Church.

Sincerely,

The Building Fund Committee [7]

Christmas

A Christmas Present to Your Church

What is lovelier than truly beautiful stained-glass windows, done in the finest medieval tradition? We have seven choice windows now, to be sure, but there are two in the nave, three in the chancel, and six in the balcony still unfinished.

To install fadeless windows of the finest hand-blown, pot-metal glass that will stand the test of centuries will be a high privilege for us all. Plans for such windows were prepared for us, at the request of your Board of Trustees, by the Willet Studios in Philadelphia, and these designs now hang in the narthex of our church. We are sure that after you have inspected them you will agree with us as to their surpassing loveliness, their worshipful quality, and the immeasurable contribution they will make to the beauty of our sanctuary.

At the congregational meeting on November 20 the trustees were authorized to proceed with the raising of funds for the completion of this work, and we believe that each one of our members will want to have a share in this Christmas gift to the Church he loves.

We do not want anyone to cut his contributions to vitally needed organizations on account of this special fund.

The cost of the proposed eleven windows will be $16,-000--a price which, after careful study, we believe to be moder-

[7] This letter, sent to 225 persons, brought a profit of over $400, reports Harold A. Nessel, pastor Epworth Methodist Church, Saginaw, Mich.

ate. No other funds are available for this purpose; the entire amount must be raised through special gifts. Will you not take your rightful share in this work of enduring significance and send us your pledge before Christmas?

A. B. Macpherson

W. H. Hudnut, Jr.

For the Session [8]

~ ~ ~

Dear Friend in Temple Church:

There is always something new and old in every Christmas. The outer situation changes, but Christmas has an unfailing power to stir into expression the best within us, "sleeping but never dead." I greet you with the spontaneous prayer of Tiny Tim, "God bless us every one."

Sunday, December 24, the day before Christmas, calls for our best in music and message. Here are our choir numbers: "Sing Noel," from an old French carol; "As Lately We Watched," by Dickinson, with incidental solo by Hazel Wells; "Sweet Little Jesus Boy," by MacGinsey, with incidental solo by Diana Gard; trio, "My Soul Doth Magnify the Lord," by Saint-Saens, to be sung by Idare Gibson, soprano, William Jackman, tenor, and Dr. George E. Steninger, baritone. My sermon theme is "Putting Christ into Christmas."

[8] Used by William H. Hudnut, Jr., pastor First Presbyterian Church, Springfield, Ill.

We trust all our members in the Bay Area will make their way to the morning church service at eleven o'clock.

The enclosed Christmas envelope is to be used for the Retired Ministers' Fund. Our Church's share in the conference total is $760. Let us make a generous response for this worthy cause.

Above all, this Christmas let us tune in with the angel chorus, worship the Babe in the manger with shepherds and sages, and then go our way with a stronger purpose than ever to make good will the ruling principle among ourselves and with all mankind.

Faithfully yours,[9]

Communion

Dear Friends and Members:

During a leave of absence from his Church a number of years ago, the Rev. Frederick W. Robertson of Brighton, England, wrote to his people a letter, beautiful in its simple faith and in its mystical appreciation of the Lord's Supper:

"By the time this may be read to you, your Communion will be over. Again, from the hands of the officiating elders, or rather, as I trust, from Christ's own pierced hand, you will have received the symbols of His sacrifice, and said, as you received Himself afresh into your hearts, 'This we do in remembrance of Thee.' Again, the Great High Priest will have brought down the bread and wine from the altar of His atonement to feed you, returning, weary from battle, but I trust victorious over evil; and in the strength of this meal may you go onward, conquering evil, and battling for the right and good and true, so as at last to have an entrance administered to you abundantly

[9] Edgar Allan Lowther, pastor Temple Methodist Church, San Francisco, Calif.

into the Kingdom, as part of the victorious 'Sacramental host of God's Elect.'"

These tender words of a minister for his people, as together they approached the table of the Lord, have been with me afresh in recent days as I have thought of you and the approaching observance of the Lord's Supper <u>next</u> Sunday morning, September 14. Our Master will be there, as always He. has been, inviting us to draw near, that He may feed us with the Bread of Life, and I trust that each of us, responsive to the Eternal "This do," will plan to assemble at this sacred hour--to turn aside that we may see what great things the Lord hath done.

Looking forward with joy to the privilege of being with you once more and sharing the Christian quest together, I am,

Faithfully your minister,[10]

~ ~ ~

Dear Friends and Fellow Members:

Not long ago I was startled in my reading by this statement: "The quality of a man's religion may be measured by the regularity of his participation in the Church's various observances of the Lord's Supper."

I should never have thought of putting it that way! For one thing, we all like to think of religion as active and practical. Micah's thoughts are our thoughts: "What doth the Lord require of thee, but to do justly, and to love mercy, and to walk humbly with thy God!" Moreover, we all know some very excellent Christians who belong to fellowships, like the Society of Friends, in which the Lord's Supper is not observed.

Nevertheless, it is a significant fact in human experience that, not uncommonly, men and women who have enriched in unusual measure the life of their day have been distinguished also for the

[10] Harold B. Kerschner, First Presbyterian Church, Poughkeepsie, N. Y.

intensity of their desire to share the sacramental observances of their Church.

After all, true religion in its various expressions is all one pattern--an all-out way of living in defense of those values to which the Master gave the last full measure of devotion. And in the communion occasion, "In remembrance," we do pledge ourselves anew, in fellowship with those who are like-minded, to those aims and purposes which are the hope of this dark world.

We shall fellowship together in the Lord's Supper next Sunday morning, September 13, at ten-forty-five. I look forward with genuine pleasure to the privilege of being with you once more, after many weeks--"With desire I have desired to eat this passover with you!"

With much appreciation of your kindness in granting us so generous a holiday, and with warm regards, I am,

Faithfully your minister,[11]

Condolence

My dear M---:

I am deeply concerned to hear of the loss which you have sustained in the death of your ----, and I wish to express to you my most sincere and profound sympathy in this time of bereavement and sorrow.

Only those who have been through such deep waters of grief and trial can fully appreciate what this experience means. I understand, and I feel for you. I pray that you may be comforted and sustained by divine consolation, and that under the weight of your sorrow you may feel the everlasting arms of the great Father.

Yours very sincerely,

[11] Harold B. Kerschner, First Presbyterian Church, Poughkeepsie, N. Y.

Dear ----:

On the anniversary of your bereavement I want you to know that your minister shares with you, in some small measure, the memories which it brings. It cannot do much to heal the pain that sorrow always leaves, but it is at least something to know that there are those who understand and sympathize with you.

There is comfort in knowing that our loved ones who have passed on, although they are beyond our sight, have entered into the glorious heritage of the redeemed, and are with Christ. Their joy and satisfaction can mitigate the sense of loss which we feel.

And there is always the solace of remembering that this separation is only temporary. Through the divine grace, we have the assurance that we shall one day meet with them again in the Father's house. And then we shall realize that the sufferings of this present time are not worthy to be compared with the glory which shall be revealed.

That you may be greatly cheered and sustained by the unfailing companionship of the sympathetic Christ is the sincere wish of

Your friend and minister,[12]

~ ~ ~

Dear Miss Collins:

Your father has just written· me of the passing of your mother. He tells us that he cabled you and that you replied. Out of a similar sorrow some years ago, I write you this note of understanding and sympathy.

It is at such a time as this that our Christian faith gives us "the victory that overcometh the world." While there is an in-

[12] This and the preceding letter are used by J. W. G. Ward, pastor First Presbyterian Church, Oak Park, Ill. The first is for the person who is away from home and therefore inaccessible for a pastoral call.

evitable sense of loss, there is at the same time a profound peace in knowing that we and all those we love are in the keeping of One whose love is as great as his power and wisdom. In our Gethsemanes, let us, like our Master, say, Father, not our will, but thine, be done. In that act of surrender, we also may have the angels of God to strengthen us.

I am sure you had faced this possibility before you decided to accept service abroad. That being true, I know you had, in the words of a sermon I read years ago, won your "victory in advance." Nevertheless, the realization that one is gone who was more precious than life itself leaves a human feeling of deep loneliness. From experience I can say that the Lord never leaves us nor forsakes us, and that Jesus, who himself knew sorrow, fulfills his promises. "I will not leave you comfortless: I will come to you."

When we lose those we love in the flesh, their character and spiritual influence assume a correspondingly greater place in our lives. It is in that sense that we can never lose those we love. The graces and ministries of your mother's life will be a growing comfort and inspiration to you. The power of her affection and sacrifices for you and the other children will become a challenge to you all to live worthily of her and thus make lasting her rich and godly life.

Helen shares with me in sincere sympathy and prayers for you. You will hear from her soon. She and the girls join me in warmest affection for you and thankfulness to God for your radiant trust in Him who doeth all things well.

Cordially yours,[13]

Easter

Dear Friends:

Easter Sunday comes on the first day of April this year. Of course, Easter Sunday is the high day of the Church Year. To

[13] J. S. Land, pastor St. Charles Avenue Presbyterian Church, New Orleans, La.

get the most out of the Easter Service, one needs to prepare for it.

So, in order to make it possible for you to get the most out of Easter this year, the official board of the Asbury Methodist Church has set aside the month of March as "Church Attendance Month" under the slogan "March to Church in March."

In these trying and difficult days, one needs all the inner strength and resources it is possible to secure. We believe that attendance at the regular services of your Church will help to meet this need.

Each person attending Asbury Church during the month of March will be asked to register his attendance. So it might be well to have a pencil in your pocket or purse. Tickets for that purpose will be provided in the church.

During this month the pastor will continue "Great Experiences in the Life of Jesus" with the following topics:

March 4 - "The Transfiguration: An Emergency Measure"

March 11 - "Gethsemane: The Strange, Lone Struggle"

March 18 - "Calvary: Victory"

March 25 - "Jerusalem: A Pageant of Triumph"

Then the series will close on Easter Sunday with "The Resurrection: Gravity Upward."

I trust that this coming Easter will bring to you an ever-deepening sense of the power of the Risen Christ.

Yours sincerely,

Parents desiring to have babies or small children baptized at Easter time are requested to communicate with the pastor not later than March 18.[14]

[14] Used by Harry L. Allen, pastor Asbury Methodist Church, Tacoma, Wash.

Dear Fellow Member:

From the very beginning of Christianity, Easter was such a holy experience that a new day of the week--Sunday--was used to remind Christians of the resurrection. It is impossible to overemphasize the spiritual meaning of Easter. Here in First Church we have always realized that this day has a divine message for all Christians.

In a very reverent and practical way, moreover, we eagerly attempt to make the Easter hope real in the hearts of people--all over the world. That is why our offering is directed specifically to "World Service." Among other causes these include: home and foreign missions, Christian education, the American Bible Society, evangelism, and hospitals and homes.

I know that you will give graciously, generously, and happily. A special envelope is enclosed for your convenience. Please use this on Easter Sunday.

Thank you so much for your loyal support of all the causes of Christianity!

Sincerely yours,[15]

Easter membership

Dear Friend:

You are one whom we believe Christ would like to have definitely enlisted in the membership of his Church. As a committee similar to that which should be functioning in every Methodist Church, particularly between now and Easter, we ask your courteous attention for a few moments now and then during the next few weeks to some thoughts which we will present in this form.

We trust that in the quiet of your own home, without any personal pressure from anyone, you will think them over

[15] G. Ray Jordan, pastor First Methodist Church, Charlotte, N. C.

carefully, realizing that in a series of general letters, every idea will not, of course, apply directly to you. If it were spring or summer and we knew of a good fishing spot, swimming hole, or berry patch, we would be a bit selfish if we did not share this knowledge--especially if there were plenty of fish, great quantities of berries, and ample room for all who wished to swim. It is in this spirit of "sharing" that we bring these thoughts to you.

We realize that many who have considerable religion have never joined the Church. But some who have been religious outside of church membership have often admitted, after they joined, that their spiritual aspirations were strengthened, they felt a closer kinship with Christ, and found their opportunities for doing good multiplied.

We want you and need you in the work of your local Methodist Church. The influence of your example in uniting openly with Christ's cause here will help Him and us to make actual the church which Theodore Parker described in these words: "The church that is to lead this century will not be a church creeping on all fours, mewling and whining, its face turned down, its eyes turned back. It must be full of the brave, manly spirit of the day, keeping also the good times of the past. . . . Let us have a church for the whole man; trust for the mind, good works for the hands, love for the heart; and, for the soul, that aspiring after perfection, that unfaltering faith in God which, like lightning in the clouds, shines brightest when elsewhere it is more dark."

Sincerely,

Chairman
The Committee on Evangelism [16]

[16] Used by John Edwin Price, pastor, Methodist Church, Sidney Center, N. Y.

Evangelism

Dear Mr. Yarbrough:

This is not a "publicity" letter; it is a personal letter to you about a very important matter. It comes to you because you have given Memorial Presbyterian Church as your preference in Oxford. You have expressed your interest in our Church, and we are glad to number you in our student congregation.

According to your church preference card, you are not a member of any church. Clearly this is not because you are indifferent either to religion or the Church. It is because you are concerned about religion, and yet have not taken the step of becoming a member of a church, that I am writing you.

Please don't misunderstand the spirit of this communication. You are no less welcome at Memorial Church because you have not joined a church. It is entirely possible that you are more loyal to the Church, and more vitally religious than many church members.

Furthermore, we do not believe that there is any magic in putting your name on a church roll. And we certainly do not believe that the Presbyterian Church is the only true branch of the Christian Church; we do recognize however that the only way to join The Church is to join a church.

We believe that the way to experience the full meaning of the Christian faith is to join the Christian movement, and to worship and serve as a full participant in it. To do so does not mean that we affirm that the Church as we see it today is all that it ought to be. Protestants recognize the imperfections of the churches, and seek to transform them from within.

On the coming two Sunday mornings Dr. Porter will be dealing with "The Inadequacy of Individual Religion" and "The Necessity of a Redemptive Society." I hope you will hear these sermons, and that you will stop in at Westminster House, 14 South

Campus Avenue, or the Manse, 410 East High Street, to talk with one of us about membership in this or your home church.

Very sincerely yours,[17]

Fellowship (youth)

Dear Bob:

This is just a little note to tell you how glad I am to welcome you into the fellowship of our Church. Of course, we receive joyfully anyone who wishes to join us, but we rejoice far more when one comes, as you have, with a whole life to give to our blessed Lord.

Now when you play a game, you want to play it just as well as you can. Certainly in playing this greatest of games--that of being a Christian--you especially wish to play at your very best. To help you in doing this, I am going to offer you a few suggestions which others, as well as myself, have found useful. A good life is made up of good habits. I hope you will make a habit of doing the following:

1. Remember always that God is very near and very eager to help you.

2. Cultivate the habit of speaking to God. Ask his help for yourself and for others and thank him for his goodness. Set aside a little time for this every morning before you go to school and every night before you go to sleep.

3. Let God speak to you each day by reading a bit in his word, especially the New Testament and the Psalms.

4. Make a habit of attending church and giving to its support.

[17] The Rev. C. Eugene Conover, director Westminster Foundation, Miami University, Oxford, Ohio.

5. Try constantly to be as kind and thoughtful and helpful to others as you would like them to be to you.

Cultivate these fine habits and you will find yourself growing in knowledge, joy, and usefulness. May God's richest blessings be yours.

Affectionately your pastor,[18]

Leadership

Dear Friend:

Don't you love to daydream about the wonderful things you could do if you had a million dollars? You'd see that Mother and Dad didn't have to work so hard; you'd give your kid sister music lessons; you'd stake Jimmy, that spunky little newsboy, to an education; you'd build a recreation room for your Sunday School--you might even include a swimming pool!

You dream on until you come down to earth with a bang --the phone is ringing: someone wants to know if you will take part on the program Sunday. You gather your scattered wits and try to think up a good excuse for refusing, meanwhile feeling rather resentful that the heart-warming glow of generosity was dispelled by such a humdrum interruption.

If only you did have a million, wouldn't you have fun making people happy, and wouldn't the folks in your Church sit up and take notice if you could make such a splendid contribution?

A contribution--a man in our Church said to the new preacher, "I have very little money to give, but my time is yours whenever you need me. Just call on me; I'll try to do anything you ask." What a giver he was! His words have become a tradition throughout the congregation.

[18] Clovis G. Chappell, Galloway Memorial Methodist Church, Jackson, Miss.

Have you ever stopped to realize that Christ never gave anyone any money? The riches of the world were his for the taking, and his to give away, yet when the poor and hungry came to him, he didn't give them money, and he rarely gave them food; he gave them love and service, and the greatest gift of all— himself.

Let's stop wishing for that million dollars! Let's stop daydreaming of the wonderful gifts we would make to our Church and our loved ones. Let's give what we have: our talents and time, our energies and enthusiasm, our love and our lives. And let's offer them without waiting to be asked for them.

Will you go to your pastor, Sunday School teacher, or superintendent, and say, "Here I am; use me"? Then you will be giving the greatest gift of all, you will be giving even as Christ gave!

Sincerely yours,[19]

Membership

Dear Friend:

This is just a brief note to tell you how glad we are to have you as a member of our congregation. I am happy personally to welcome you into the fellowship of our Church. We sincerely hope that you will feel at home with us. We trust also that you will find in your church life a continual source of inspiration and usefulness. That you may do this, I am going to venture a few brief suggestions.

First, make a business of your religion. So many people have no religious technique. Give the Church a central place in your life. Give it the same serious consideration that you give your home and your business. Support it by your means. In so far as possible, be a part of its school. Attend its services of worship. Remember that a good life is made up of good habits.

[19] This message, written by Edwina Sanders, is reprinted from *Church Business,* a publication of the Duplex Envelope Company, Richmond, Va.

Second, seek to commend your Church to your loved ones and to your friends. There are many today who think and speak slightingly of the Church. The seat of the scornful is full, also the seat of the mournful. But it is your privilege and mine to be among those who help and believe and encourage. This we can do by being loyal to our Church.

Third, find at least a brief moment each day to read a bit out of God's word. Cultivate the habit of prayer. In so doing, you will find yourself growing at once in usefulness and joy.

Finally, if at any time there is any service that the pastors of this Church can render, please command us. It is not only our business to help you in every way possible, but it is our high privilege.

Again extending to you the heartiest of welcomes, I am

Sincerely your pastor,[20]

~ ~ ~

Dear Friends:

May I add to the public welcome you were extended last Sunday my own warm personal greeting? I am happy to see you join our church family. I firmly believe St. Paul Methodist Church has a unique religious service to render you and through you a service to all who make Muskogee their home.

As your pastor, permit me to make a few suggestions. In the observance of them, I believe you will make most effective your church membership, and will make your personal religious life one of happiness and great satisfaction to you.

LEAD A LIFE OF PRAYER! Have some form of daily devotions. Maintain a fellowship with God at all times; take Christ

[20] Clovis G. Chappell, Galloway Memorial Methodist Church, Jackson, Miss.

into your work, your home, your recreation, your everyday experiences. I suggest the use of the "Upper Room," a book of devotions that you may secure quarterly at the church for five cents a copy.

ATTEND CHURCH REGULARLY! In this way your Church can serve you and you will be giving your moral support to its program. For your own sake, a good rule to follow is: ATTEND CHURCH EVERY SUNDAY!

SERVE THROUGH YOUR CHURCH! Your Church needs you, and there is a place for everyone. If you are to grow spiritually, active participation is necessary; furthermore, sustained interest and loyalty to Christ will develop as a consequence of such service.

Do not at any time neglect any of these, and remember that your pastor and those in charge are always ready to serve you. Do not hesitate to come and talk over any matter of interest to you or to the Church.

Praying God's blessings on you, and asking that you keep us and the Church always in your prayers, I am,

Cordially your pastor,[21]

~ ~ ~

Dear Friend:

This is to express to you again the cordial welcome of your pastor and of the warmhearted congregation of which you are now a member.

Your impression of our Church has been gained from other people. Now other people's opinion of it will be gained in

[21] Thomas H. Raper, St. Paul Methodist Church, Muskogee, Okla.

part from you. Your loyalty, your devotion, your enthusiasm, will be a major factor in someone's choice of a church and his belief in the Church.

One of our Methodist bishops has said: "Joining the Church of Christ is something different from joining a lodge or other secular organization. It is a matter of dedication, the giving of one's self and the giving of one's substance. Indeed the giving of one's self to the work of Christ is basic. It is the reason for our joining the Church at all. The Church is composed of people who have caught the vision of the better kind of life, the better kind of world that God the Heavenly Father desires in the interest of his children. We have committed ourselves to a program and a way of life."

There are ways by which we can express our loyalty and develop it so that our love for the Church becomes a deep and abiding passion.

1. I will attend the services of worship. "And Jesus, . . . as his custom was, . . . went into the synagogue on the sabbath day." He made it a habit. We turn to him for strength and guidance and inner poise in these troubled days.

2. I will pray for my Church. In such days as these prayer is greatly needed. Your minister, church officials, organizational leaders, everyone with responsibility, greatly needs the interest of your prayers. Let the Church be remembered in your private prayers and in your expression of thanks at the table.

3. I will serve my Church. Our Lord recognized that not everyone has the same talent. But each of us can do at least one thing that will help in the total task of the Church.

4. I will pay of my money to the Church. When we attend the public means of grace, pray for our Church in private, and render it such services as we can, our gifts have fuller and deeper meaning than before, because the value of a dollar in a

church treasury is more than a hundred cents. It is prayer and purpose and personality, service and sacrifice, vision.

Sincerely yours,[22]

Opinion survey

Dear Members of Linden Avenue:

As you know, our Church has voted to select a site, near the geographical center of Memphis, for our new church home.

One hundred and twenty-five of our young people met in the Keystone classroom March 11, when Mrs. Coppedge presented to them our general plans for the future. You see, we realize that they will play a large part in leading and conducting the work of Linden Avenue in the future, as well as in paying for the maintenance and obligations of erecting a new church home.

These young people expressed themselves freely as to what they desire in recreational advantages: an outdoor swimming pool, bowling alleys, dance floor, motion picture projector, and a wooded picnic grounds. It was their desire to have the educational rooms as a part of the church proper, with the recreational division separate. They want the sanctuary to be cathedral-like, with a belfry and chimes.

We would greatly appreciate a word from you that would serve as your vote of confidence in our efforts. We would also like to have any comments, or suggestions, concerning a new site and what you would like in a new church. All plans, of course, would have to be approved by the official board and a congregational vote, but we certainly want you to enter into our plans and thinking.

Enclosed is a postal card on which to express your ideas. We suggest you mail it in an envelope to speed delivery.

Cordially,[23]

[22] This message, printed in a leaflet, was written by Ronald E. Terry, pastor First Methodist Church, Cheyenne, Wyo.

[23] Howard Thomas Wood, pastor Linden Avenue Christian Church, Memphis, Tenn.

Dear Member:

This is not a general newsletter to the entire member-ship of the Church. It is going to only 100 of our families. It is therefore important, even though it is mimeographed, and I trust you will read every word of it.

The purpose of this letter is to see if we cannot interest you--and your family--in the work of the Church enough to as-sume certain definite responsibilities during the month of Janu-ary. I am asking the hundred to whom this letter goes to act next month as if no one belonged to this Church but them. Therefore, if you do not intend to carry on the work of the Church, it will not be done. NOW--THAT IS THE CHALLENGE. Will you accept it?

If you are interested enough to want to hear more about the plan, please sign the enclosed card and return it at once. At the dinner meeting (plates will be 50 cents each)--January 4, 1945, at 7 P. M.--we will make our plans. If you are interested and will co-operate, and still cannot come to the meeting, please indicate that on the card.

Here are some of the things we want you to do:

What would you do if you were running this Church? As president of the W. S. C. S.? Or chair-man of the Board? Or superintendent of the Church School? Or even pastor? Well, that is what we want to talk about.

Among other things, we want you to serve as hosts to everyone who comes to church during this month, some to visit the sick, others to visit the new people in Gainesville, and a special committee to go to the hospital twice a week. And on and on. We will decide just how much and what kind of work we can do.

200

As your pastor, I am gratified that the work is progressing so smoothly. But as a sincere Christian, I can see that most of us are still just playing at the job. I want you to help me this month of January really <u>to put First Church to work.</u>

Will you join hands with me and see HOW MUCH WE CAN DO for the Church and our Lord?

Expectantly yours,[24]

Parents

Dear Mrs. Sowers:

Last Sunday your son John worshiped with us at First Methodist Church, Fresno, and signed a card giving us your name that I might personally write this letter to you.

I am always happy to see out-of-town boys in our services, and I am sure you will be glad to know that your son is looking in this direction even when he is away from home. If there is anything we can do for him while he is with us, I hope you will feel free to write to me.

I am enclosing a copy of our bulletin. If you are a Methodist and have a Methodist hymnal I suggest you look up the hymns and the responsive reading, and in this way share the service with us and with your loved one.

Sincerely yours,[25]

～　～　～

Dear Mrs. Werner:

I am writing to express to you my sincere congratulations upon the outstanding achievements attained by your son Bob during the recent summer leadership camp at Turner Falls.

[24] Jack Anderson, pastor First Methodist Church, Gainesville, Fla.
[25] Theodore Henry Palmquist, pastor First Methodist Church, Fresno, Calif.

He was elected chairman of the worship committee and was active in directing various recreational events. Most important of all, he was elected district representative to the State Council for the coming year.

You have every reason to be proud of Bob, and this note is just to tell you that I, too, appreciate the outstanding work he is doing.

Cordially yours,

Prospective members

Dear Mr. and Mrs. Henry:

Bob Park has suggested that I invite you people to our Church--an invitation that I am very happy to give.

We want to offer to you the facilities of our Church and its staff in any way in which we may be of service. We look forward to the pleasure of having you worship with us at our regular services, which are held at eleven o'clock each Sunday morning, and hope that you will feel encouraged to participate in the varied activities of the Church as they are announced in our weekly bulletin.

The Church School meets each Sunday at eleven o'clock, with a nursery school for three- and four-year-olds, and departments for all ages up through juniors (twelve years of age). The departments for children too young to attend church continue until noon, at which time the worship service promptly adjourns. This permits parents to attend church while their small children are being given educationally sound training in our splendid children's school. Provision is made for children under three years of age, but old enough to walk, in the Toddler's Room.

Classes for adults and older youth meet each Sunday at ten o'clock, and three splendid youth groups for young people of junior high, senior high, college, and employed ages meet Sunday evenings.

We are taking the liberty of adding your name for a short period to our mailing list.

Members of our congregation will be in touch with you in the near future to invite you personally to our Church. Whenever you are in attendance at our services, I hope you will give me the privilege of meeting you.

Yours very truly,[26]

~ ~ ~

Dear Friend:

A noted world traveler once told me: "Wherever I go, I know I can buy a familiar little yellow box containing a refill for my camera. I wish my Church were equally solicitous for my soul."

If you have talked with as many people in this community as I have, I know you will agree with me that many of them have drifted away from the Church or have never joined with it simply because they have never realized just how solicitous the Church is for their welfare.

Don't misunderstand me! By "solicitous" I don't mean that Forest Hills Church engages in the constant pursuit of its members for their souls' sake. It by no means acts as a millstone of propriety around their necks, nor does it attempt to play Mrs. Grundy to the community.

But I honestly believe that it offers you something you are missing if you are without it--something you can get nowhere else in life--something you need to live a life of the fullest and happiest kind.

It offers you the fellowship of a congenial group--people you will be glad to know and proud to have as friends.

[26] William Atkinson Young, pastor First Presbyterian Church, Peoria, Ill.

It offers you an opportunity to enter into an important phase of the life of this community--its religious life.

It offers you a spiritual home--a place where you can partake in the worship of God and get the inspiration and the stimulus so necessary to your daily life. Only a church can give you this—and only a church can be, in this way, "solicitous for your welfare."

Please consider this letter a personal invitation to you and your family to join us next Sunday at eleven o'clock. Consider it, if you like, an opportunity to make me prove the points I have outlined here. My hope is that one visit will lead to another --and that you will decide to join with us permanently at Forest Hills Community Church.

Cordially and faithfully,

Pastor [27]

Stewardship

Dear Friends:

"Better late than never" is a saying you have often heard. But it is only the first half of the proverb. The rest reads, "Better never late."

At the request of the Finance Committee of the Church Council, I am writing to you and 122 other members of our Church who have either given nothing to its support since June 1, or have been quite irregular in their giving.

I realize that some of you have been in the habit of paying toward the support of our Church on a yearly basis, and that no doubt you are planning soon to make that annual payment.

[27] Used by permission of A. B. Dick Company, Chicago, Ill.

I realize that others of you have been away during the summer months and will soon catch up on the weekly envelopes you have missed.

I think, too, that some of you have been just a little careless in turning in your envelopes, though all the while you have had the good of our Church at heart.

I know also that some contribute when they come, but not through the envelopes.

It is a big help, however, when ALL our members contribute REGULARLY! It makes the work of the church council so much easier when the men know fairly accurately just how much we can depend upon to meet each month's bills.

Will you, therefore, help? How? I suggest--

1. Use your envelopes. If you contribute without them, we have no means of knowing that you contribute and can give you no credit.

2. Use them regularly. Fill them each week, according as GOD HAS PROSPERED YOU, whether you can come to church that week or not. This habit, once formed, will keep you from falling behind in your support of our Church.

Remember, we no longer seek pledges from you, nor do we trouble you every three months with a statement as to how much you owe on your pledge. We depend now upon your realization of the fact that OUR CHURCH is YOUR CHURCH, and therefore should receive your support.

Will you, then, please "catch up" and stay "caught up"? You'll feel better, and your church council certainly will, too.

Sincerely yours,[28]

[28] Reprinted from *Church Business*, a publication of the Duplex Envelope Company, Richmond, Va.

Dear First Baptist Friend:

What a privilege it is to be your pastor! I appreciate more than you know the hearty manner in which you are rallying to my ministry.

A wise pastor will kindly and lovingly show his people what the Bible teaches about giving.

We Should Give Joyfully: "God loveth a cheerful giver." 2 Cor. 9:7.

We Should Give Regularly: "Upon the first day of the week let every one of you lay by him in store, as God hath prospered him." 1 Cor. 16:2.

We Should Give Proportionately: "Thou shalt truly tithe all the increase of thy seed." Deut. 14:22. (Have you ever tried the joy of tithing? God has promised spiritual blessings to those who are faithful to him.) Join me in a three-months trial.

Why Should We Give? Because: "Christ . . . hath loved us, and hath given himself for us." Eph. 5:2.

Why Should We Give to the Local Church? "That there may be meat in mine house, . . . saith the Lord." Mal. 3:10.

Why Should We Give to Missions? Because Jesus commanded it: "Go ye into all the world, and preach the gospel to every creature." Mark 16: 15.

I am especially anxious for every member of the Church to know the joy of regular giving through the envelopes. Fill out your pledge card and BRING it on Sunday, October 28, but first pray mightily that God will bless our mutual service for him in this historic Church.

Faithfully your pastor,[29]

[29] Hillyer H. Straton, First Baptist Church, Malden, Mass.

Dear Friend:

Statesmen, writers, commentators, and laymen have been increasingly recognizing the need for spiritual awakening. Whether this growing recognition is in itself a spiritual awakening is not clear. What IS clear, I think, is the implied challenge to the Church--to OUR Church and to OUR members--to "Keep the Church moving forward," as Bishop Tucker phrases it.

Thinking men and women again regard service and sacrifice as virtues to be practiced--after a too-long period of neglect. These virtues have found expression in refugee relief, Red Cross, aid in defense of freedom, aroused patriotism--to name a few. Clearly, in this challenge to the Church, there is opportunity for its members to exercise these virtues--to practice Christian stewardship.

Every church member, by the exercise of service and sacrifice, is rewarded with enhanced spiritual stamina, with a happier heart, with a more buoyant conscience, with a sweeter serenity of the soul.

Membership in a Christian Church is a privilege to be appreciated and preserved; and the practice of the stewardship ideal implies that the Church shall be supported by all its members on a broad democratic base. Our Church stakes its existence and its growth on its ability to win and hold its members to the practice of this Christian stewardship.

As but one expression of this stewardship, each member is asked annually to pledge in advance a definite sum for the support of the Church. Annually, a time is set aside for the conduct of the Every Member Canvass. This is a time for reviewing and evaluating what the Church has done--for laying plans to "Keep the Church moving forward." It is a time for ALL members, acting in unison, to consider whether the Church is meeting its challenge.

The vestry has designated the week of November 3 for the Every Member Canvass. Within a few days you will be sent the treasurer's budget and report. The vestry is preparing an outline of church activities and plans which will reach you soon. I ask that you read these carefully. Their purpose is to inform you about your Church.

Faithfully your friend and rector,[30]

~ ~ ~

Dear Sir:

A powerful song, often included in the repertoire of great artists, has it:

"Give me some men
Who are stout-hearted men
Who will fight for the right they adore!
Give me some men
Who are stout-hearted men
And I'll soon give you ten thousand more!" [31]

With due apologies to the author of those lines, allow me to paraphrase them:

Give me some men
Who are stout-hearted men
Who will work and sweat
For the liquidation of our debt!
Give me some men
Who are stout-hearted men
And we'll soon our ten thousand get!

[30] R. H. Baker, The Church of the Redeemer, Baltimore, Md. This letter, which was one in a series, was one of the 1941 winners in a competition sponsored by the Direct Mail Advertising Association, Inc.

[31] By Oscar Hammerstein II. Used by permission.

I am asking you to be one of at least twenty-five teams of two who will meet with me immediately after the second worship service next Sunday for cards and instructions.

It is the plan not to have over ten cards for each team. Your "prospects" will have been notified that you are calling Sunday afternoon and asked to be at home and to have their decisions reached.

I shall plan to see you at the second worship service, which starts at 10:50 A. M., and I shall do my best, by way of sermon and announcement, to make your work easy for you. Also, I shall see to it that you have cards and instructions and are on your way home to dinner by 12:10 at the latest. Knowing the men to whom these letters are being sent, I am taking the liberty of assigning the teams and you can make arrangements with your partner regarding the time you will start out.

Please keep in mind that we do not plan to have another every-member canvass this year, except to call on the new members of our Church who have not as yet made a pledge.

Thanks for your co-operation.

Most sincerely,[32]

~ ~ ~

OH, COME TO (the aid of) THE CHURCH IN THE RED!

There's a church that is white on the hilltop,
  There's a church that is brown in the vale.
But the church in the red, my dear brethren,
  Is the subject of my little tale.

[32] Homer J. R. Elford, pastor First Methodist Church, Grand Forks, N. D.

I know there's the rent, and the groceries,
    And the balance you use to raise Ned.
But--come! raise your pledge to the budget,
    For who wants a church in the red?

Our forefathers built it so bravely.
    You can't do it staying in bed.
Moral--"Stir up the gift that is in you,"
    And we won't have a church in the red.

Oh, pay-up, pay-up, pay-up your pledge
    to the church house.
    I hope nothing more need be said.
Let each of us budge for the budget,
    And we'll not have our church in the red!

The above was written by the Rev. John D. Clinton of Fayette, Iowa, and it fits our situation here so well that we are using it.

It is very true that our Church is "in the red." It is likewise true that if all past-due pledges were paid to date, and if some who do not pledge would come to the assistance of their Church, we would be "out of the red."

Our expenses are extremely heavy during these days of cold weather and short daylight hours. Will you not help us bring our Church "out of the red" and "into the black"?

Sincerely yours,

The Finance Committee

By_____

Chairman [33]

---

[33] Used by A. Norman Evans, pastor Austin Avenue Methodist Church, Waco, Tex. Poem reprinted by permission of the author.

Dear Member and Friend:

Tomorrow we begin the last quarter of our fiscal year. In looking over our financial situation, we find some improvement over last year, and for that we are grateful. There is disappointment, however, in the fact that some who can well afford to do so are not supporting their Church as they should.

How many people find it difficult to run their household on $200 a month? How far do you suppose $383.68 (our total budget income for June) will go toward paying the expense of a great Church like ours?

We give this word of explanation
For your kind consideration
Of the financial situation
  In our church.
We need full co-operation
Of this splendid congregation
Or we'll be, sans reservation,
  In the lurch!

We can ill afford cessation
Of your regular month's duration,
  Don't you see?
Since our bills take no vacation,
We must have continuation
Of our income--sound equation,
  You'll agree.

So good people of high station,
Please keep up your reputation,
Give us your collaboration
  On the spot.
Then we'll have a celebration,
Based on your kind ministration

211

And, with a great anticipation,
THANKS A LOT!

Sincerely yours,

The Finance Committee,[34]

~ ~ ~

Dear Friend:

One day Thomas Jefferson and some friends were on a horseback ride. They came to a swollen stream where stood a traveler in need of a lift.

The president's companions rode into the stream and across. When Jefferson rode up, the traveler asked him for a ride across the creek. His request was granted; and when they were on the other side, Thomas Jefferson said to him, "I am curious to know why you asked me instead of my companions for this favor."

The reply is significant. "You see," said he, "there are some personalities which seem to say 'no' and the others seem to say 'yes.' Theirs said 'no' and yours said 'yes.'"

This is to tell you that a goodly number of our members said "yes" to our Every Member Enrollment invitation last Sunday afternoon. Subscriptions totaled approximately $2,700 when the final count was made.

Believing that all of you are affirmative personalities, we are giving you the opportunity to say "YES" at the Sunday school and church services next Sunday, and in the afternoon from two to three o'clock.

[34] Used by A. Norman Evans while he was pastor of McFarlin Memorial Church, Norman, Okla.

212

I like the Presbyterian way, don't you, of a brief period of emphasis on finances, leaving the remainder of the year free for worship, fellowship, and other values of the Kingdom?

Very sincerely yours,[35]

～ ～ ～

Dear Friend:

Since writing our various letters with regard to the Every Member Canvass for 19-- we have not been favored by you with a word in reply which would afford some idea of your intention for your own Church in the program it fervently hopes to follow as God's mandate in the year ahead.

We do not feel that this is merely your way of letting us know that you have no interest in--shall we say "God's Battle-Front?"--because we know that with your Christian background you realize full well that what happens there affects your life's foundations too profoundly. But today, complacency is too real an "enemy" on this "front."

Therefore, we are moved to ask you three questions, and we would greatly appreciate it if you would be so kind as to make a prompt reply:

1) Do you desire further information regarding this Canvass, involving an explanation of its purpose and why your part in it is so vitally important? Is there anything that has been approved in the Congregational Meeting in your name to which you would offer objection? You have a right to express yourself in this way, you know.

2) Can you help us with any suggestion as to how we can improve the Church's service to you as a member and to all it hopes to serve? As a member of the Church you have

[35] Mitchell S. Epperson, pastor First Presbyterian Church, Ada, Okla.

a right to express any constructive criticism on any phase of the work which you feel elicits judgment on your part.

3) Within a few weeks a volunteer group will take the field to close the Canvass, which is still short of its goal by some $4,000. Would you prefer to discuss in confidence with some members of this group on a personally assigned visit to you any or all of these matters? We feel that your willingness to do so would, of itself, be a worthy contribution to the better world we are bent upon creating with loyal, remembering hearts and the substance which God has so abundantly provided.

Very cordially yours,

Every Member Canvass Committee
The Messrs. Gulden, Herrlich, and
Dahmer [36]

~ ~ ~

My Christian Comrades:

Which of these words do you like better--FOR or FROM?

Your answer will make a good deal of difference in your life, particularly in your happiness and success.

If life is a FOR word, an opportunity to live FOR something worth-while, then you will have the joy and thrill of sharing in noble enterprises that help mankind. If you measure life in terms of what is taken FROM you, you will be miserable.

Take the matter of giving. If giving is a FROM word, something taken FROM you, giving will be a hardship. But if giving is a FOR word, giving FOR great causes, FOR the church, FOR the help of little children, FOR the encouragement of

[36] Used by Paul Scherer, pastor Evangelical Lutheran Church of the Holy Trinity, New York City.

youth, FOR the great enterprises of Christ, FOR the winning of the world to our Lord, then giving becomes one of life's outstanding privileges.

Soon you will be given an opportunity to sign your church pledge.

Is the Church taking something FROM you? Or--

Are you giving something FOR your Lord?

The amount of your pledge and the spirit in which you make it will be your answer.

Sincerely yours,[37]

~ ~ ~

Dear Friend:

Have you heard this one? A Negro preacher announced from the pulpit that a brother had neglected to lock the door of his chicken house the night before, with the result that most of his fowls were missing. "I has my s'picions who stole dem chickens," said the parson, "and I also b'lieves dat sech a low-down pusson ain' noways likely t' put money in de collection plate dat will now be passed." The result was a record-breaking collection!

The pastor viewed it with approval and continued: "Now, bredr'en, I don' want yo' dinner spoilt by wonderin' where dat brothah lives dat don' lock his chickens up. Dat brothah jes don' exist. He is jes' a parable fo' pu'pose ob finances."

We haven't had to go that far here in Westminster--yet! You will be glad to know that your church home is keeping

[37] This letter, written by the Rev. Ryland Knight, is reprinted from *Church Business*, a publication of the Duplex Envelope Company, Richmond, Va.

very much on the job these busy days. And we would like to think that while you are away from Rochester you think of this as your church home and are interested in what is happening here.

Enclosed is the folder outlining our financial needs for the coming year. Doesn't it give you a genuine satisfaction to feel that you are a partner of our program here? I can readily realize that you are doubtless attending some church in your present community, and contributing toward its support. But would not you like also to send us a token of your share in what we are attempting to do in Rochester?

A pledge card is enclosed. We are to have our annual Loyalty Sunday on February 25. At the service I should like to be able to report that we have heard from our out-of-town members. You can make this possible by signing the card and sending it right back to me.

Be assured that you are ever carried in our thought and prayers.

Faithfully yours,[38]

Stewardship (four-letter campaign)

My dear Friends:

Let me tell you a story. During the general excitement of the Barnum's Museum fire it was reported that a huge Bengal tiger leaped from a second-story window to the sidewalk. Some spectators stampeded in terror; others froze helplessly in their tracks while policemen banged away ineffectively with their pistols.

It was then that Fireman Denham picked up his ax, confronted the beast, and killed it with a mighty blow to the head. By this time "fully awakened," he ran into the blazing building, carried out the Fat Lady--who weighed more than

[38] Gordon W. Mattice, pastor Westminster Church, Rochester, N. Y.

216

400 pounds--and returned to rescue two children and the wooly-headed Albino Woman. Because John Denham could best be described as a quiet sort of fellow who placidly plied his trade as a stage carpenter when he wasn't running with Hose Company No. 15, probably no one was more surprised than he at his amazing response to the emergency of the moment.

One never knows his strength until he puts it to the test. You have done a perfectly splendid piece of work in beautifying our sanctuary and church. It is a joy to be a minister here. Your co-operation is wonderful. So--I make bold to ask your advice on something very near my heart and yours. With the remaining debt of our rebuilding fund so nearly liquidated, don't you think we could supply the needed funds to wipe it out entirely on Easter Sunday morning?

When I became pastor of Endion Church, Duluth, they had been carrying a $5,000 debt so long that they had spent $9,000 in interest. Don't you suppose we can slay that tiger and kill him once and for all on Easter of this very year?

Wonderingly yours,

~ ~ ~

My dear Friends:

Last week your minister wrote you about the possibility of slaying a certain tiger. Talks with many people in the Church indicate an almost unanimous sentiment in favor of killing the beast at once. The government is urging all individuals and churches as well as companies to "pay your debts off this year." In the case of churches, the government does not tax individuals for the payment made to churches.

Here is our situation in a nutshell: The total cost of rebuilding and refurnishing was $33,470, of which $30,000 has been subscribed (including $800 from Penny-a-Meal banks).

217

That leaves a balance of only $3,470 yet to raise to be "Debt free in '43."

What would it take to slay that tiger:

A few $100 gifts
Twenty $50 gifts
Thirty $25 gifts
One hundred $10 gifts
Two hundred fifty $5 gifts or less

Well, my good friends, your marvelous response to everything your new minister has suggested has led the Finance Committee and the Official Board to say "Flash the green light; let's kill the tiger now!"

Easter Sunday, with two identical services, one at 9:15 and one at 10:45, bids fair to be the most victorious Easter in the history of our Church. Just take the card and look it over carefully and prayerfully. Then let us each select the highest bracket he is capable of handling and check it off. Then sign it and bring it to one of the two great services for A DAY OF VICTORY.

Confidently yours,

~ ~ ~

My dear Friends:

This is Holy Week. It is not too much to say that never before in the history of the world have so many people been turning wistfully toward the Church for newer fortitude and courage to meet a world that has gone quite mad. God help us to be worthy interpreters of the Christ who gave his all--his life --for sin-sick men, and out of the ashes of his great sacrifice rose again victorious over death on Easter morn.

Your minister was happy and inspired last Sunday at the sight of that magnificent audience that packed the church

218

to the back walls. People love to come into that beautiful sanctuary where they can really worship God. Now for the final effort to clear it of all debt. How eagerly we shall await the final report of what Easter Sunday shall bring forth. Do you share my faith that we can do it? We can, that is, if each and every one of us does his utmost.

> I believe we can do it!
> Down with the tiger now!
> Strike your blow at one of the
> Two victorious services Easter morn!

Yours in absolute confidence,

~ ~ ~

My dear Friends:

Momentous news! Mrs. Weber was just in to report: "As a result of Sunday's collection, I just paid $2,300 in cash on the $3,500 note at the bank." Yes sir--you splendid people gave that tiger a blow on the head that sent him sprawling. He is not clear dead, but he is an awful sick tiger! There is $1,200 left to pay, with $200 in good pledges, which brings it down to $1,000, and a number of you that did not get your gifts in Sunday that we confidently expect to hear from yet. Isn't that remarkable?

What to do now? What do you think of sending the banks out again to get a Penny-a-Meal per family for just four short months? That would enable us to bury the tiger on September 1 with a funeral ceremony of such a happy nature that I'll wager even the tiger would have a smile on his face in his last long sleep of death!

Your animal-killing pastor,[39]

[39] This series of four letters was used by Lewis L. Dunnington, pastor First Methodist Church, Iowa City, Iowa, who reported: "The mortgage was burned at our annual harvest home dinner on November 2, 1943."

Sunday school

My dear ----:

So you brought a NEW MEMBER to Sunday School! That's great! It indicates that you wish to share good things with others. Regular attendance at Sunday School is a great help to boys and girls. Try to find more members. You may bring someone who later will be a great person with a big job! So go out and get him or her. We certainly appreciate your services and wish you the best of luck.

Sincerely yours,

~ ~ ~

My dear ----:

So you were at Sunday School every Sunday last month! That's great! It shows that you are faithful and dependable. And a good job is usually waiting for the boy or girl who has a reputation for being dependable and faithful.

I hope that you will make the same record this month, next month, and throughout the year--and for years to come! (One Plymouth pupil has a perfect attendance record for thirteen years.) Luck to YOU!

Yours sincerely,[40]

~ ~ ~

Dear Parents:

We are sending a Christmas letter to all the parents of the Church School children at St. Alban's. Mrs. Miller and I wish all of you a very merry Christmas.

[40] This and the preceding letter, written by J. H. Howard of the church school of Plymouth Congregational Church, Los Angeles, Calif., are reprinted from *Church Business,* a publication of the Duplex Envelope Company, Richmond, Va.

As our Church School Goes into the new secular year, we are asking all parents to co-operate with us in making our Church School an even finer one. You can help us.

We have on our staff nine trained teachers who are dynamic and interesting; we have a service of worship which is a real "Junior Church," and which prepares the youngster for the full status which he reaches when he is confirmed; and we have a session which is long enough to allow for adequate instruction. We are limited by our small space and our inadequate facilities for the very young, although children of five years have been quite happy with us.

Here is what you can do:

1) Be interested enough in the Church School to ask the children what they have learned each Sunday. You will be surprised at how intelligent they are and how modern and Christian their knowledge is.

2) Get them to us on time by stirring up their interest in what they are learning. We have fun at Church School; it is geared to the children, and there is a spirit of Christian worship and intelligent teaching.

3) Let them know that our 9:15 A.M. opening period is for the purpose of having a real "Junior Church" and a forty-minute class period. We are through at 10:40. Because we allow more time, we can be more thorough than any other school in this area.

4) Let them be proud of their Church School; remind them that their Vicar is Professor of Christian Education at the Church Divinity School of the Pacific, and Chairman of the Department of Education for the Diocese of California.

5) For those over twelve years, encourage them to be confirmed, keep them interested in Church School until they are through high school, let them join the "Bishop Parsons Club,"

and plan to send them to the Diocesan Summer Conference in June. There is much that depends on you.

Sincerely,[41]

Thanksgiving

Dear Friend:

> "Count your many blessings,
> Name them one by one.
> And it will surprise you
> What the Lord hath done."

We have all sung this gospel song many, many times, and how appropriate it is for this season of thanksgiving! We have so much for which to be thankful! It would take much more space and time than I have here to list God's blessings which have come to all of us during this year. How fine it is when we all stop for a little time and consider God's generosity.

This letter is not designed to ask for money. Nor is it to make any special announcement. It is simply a letter from your pastor in which he wants to express his thanksgiving for the grand Church which he serves and the fine people who compose it, and also to extend the best of wishes for the Thanksgiving Season.

Most of us will be going home or having friends and relatives as guests for the day. Thanksgiving is a joyous occasion. Let us this year remember that God is to be the center of the celebration. It is to Him we give thanks!

In keeping with the season we are having a special Thanksgiving service Wednesday evening (tomorrow) at 7:30 P.M. We shall be happy if you can join us in this special service

---

[41] Randolph Crump Miller, vicar St. Alban's Episcopal Church, Albany, Calif.

of thanksgiving and prayer. The sermon theme will be "Giving Thanks in Days Like These."

Enclosed you will find a copy of last Sunday's Thanksgiving sermon. It comes to you with the wish that your Thanksgiving will be the most enjoyable one you have shared. Mrs. Rupert joins me in these thanksgiving greetings.

Sincerely yours,[42]

~ ~ ~

Dear Mr. McNitt:

The first Thanksgiving of the Pilgrim Fathers welled from the hearts of men who were determined that liberty and freedom should live . . . that we might worship as we please . . . that we should express our gratitude to God.

We are thankful for the country in which we live . . . We are thankful for our friends . . . friends who have enabled us to carry on the program of the Church and thus extend Christianity into the lives of countless persons.

We hope you have enjoyed as happy relations in your church work as we have enjoyed in working with you. For your devotion, your loyalty, and your prayers we are truly thankful.

Cordially yours,

Welcome to teachers

To the Teachers of ----

We believe that this is a strategic year in the course of history, and we are taking the liberty of asking your co-operation with the churches of this city to help make ---- a better com-

[42] Used by Hoover Rupert while he was pastor of the Methodist church in Thayer, Kan.

munity, morally and spiritually. We all know that the integrity of our nation cannot be maintained without religion.

We believe that your example in religious precepts will encourage young people to become interested in the churches of our city. We also feel that there ought to be co-operation of the home, school, and Church in establishing and following Christian standards.

Each of us has a little plant called reverence that needs watering once a week in church. Our hectic lives need this association to keep alive and maintain reverence for God in this great land of ours. We do not lose our religion by a blowout; usually it is just a slow leak.

There is a great advance movement in all Christian brotherhoods to help people to see the need of coming back to our churches with their families. How can we expect the blessing of God if we neglect worship in the house of God?

We extend to you a most hearty welcome in Christian fellowship. If you have no church home, if you should like to teach or help in the work of the Church, we will try to find a place for you.

Sincerely in earnest, I am,

I Cor. 9:15-23 [43]

Worship

Dear Friend and Parishioner:

This Sunday will be the first in a new year. Let us start it right--in God's House--asking for God's blessing!

[43] Reprinted from *Church Business,* a publication of the Duplex Envelope Company, Richmond, Va.

For over three thousand years God has been asking mankind to keep his day holy--to set aside one day in seven for worship.

The world at large has rejected his plea. The world was convinced it could build a better kingdom than God could. We know now how completely it has failed.

Some of us laugh at the church-going founders of our republic. (Washington would not let even company keep him from church.) But our ridicule comes with poor grace. With a faith larger than their faults, our church-going ancestors wrested freedom from tyranny, turned a wilderness into a nation. Are we doing as much? Are we serious in wanting to hold what they won? Do we really want to safeguard civilization? What religion did once, it can do again.

Let us not fool ourselves with a counterfeit. Thoughts about God, when reading or writing, working or playing, in themselves do not constitute worship any more than thoughts alone constitute anything. A man who day after day stayed at home and did no more than think about his business, would be a failure.

Let us not fool ourselves. We either reject or accept God's weekly call to worship. There is no half way.

Sickness or some emergency can keep us at home. But if we want to believe that we are earnest--if we want God to believe it, too--then it must be the kind of sickness or emergency that would keep us from business or some social engagement.

Why not try God's way? God cannot be wrong. Why not give his way a good trial? Why not resolve to be present in the House of Prayer every Sunday--God willing, God giving us the strength to be there?

God bless you and yours! May he help you this year to make the worship of him no longer a task, but a wonderfully uplifting source of guidance and power. He will do so if you ask him.

Hoping to see you and yours Sunday, I am,

Faithfully your rector,[44]

Miscellaneous

"Central Calling to Central's Own

Away from Home"

Dear Friends:

There is such a thing as "selective hearing." That is, one can learn to hear precisely what he wants to hear--even despite the most distracting disturbances.

It is not easy to master such an accomplishment, but the rewards and satisfactions deriving from proficiency in the art are vastly worth while.

For example, have you ever noticed how promptly a mother hears the cry or call of her child--even amidst the noisiest merrymaking or the most alluring music? Most of the company may be quite oblivious to all but their immediate obsession, when suddenly the young mother rises quickly to leave the room, saying, "Excuse me, please. I hear my child."

Or the trained mechanic who immediately detects the slightest knock or telltale vibration in his machine, regardless of the roar of the motor or the clang of competing sounds?

Or the coast guardsman who catches the call of distress above the deafening thunders of the storm?

[44] This letter, written by the Rev. Carolus R. Webb, is reprinted from *Church Business,* the publication of the Duplex Envelope Company, Richmond, Va.

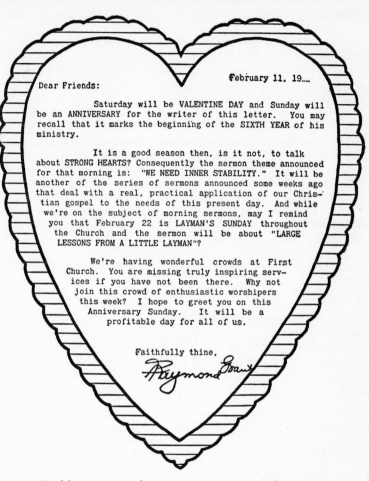

Dear Friends:

February 11, 19....

Saturday will be VALENTINE DAY and Sunday will be an ANNIVERSARY for the writer of this letter. You may recall that it marks the beginning of the SIXTH YEAR of his ministry.

It is a good season then, is it not, to talk about STRONG HEARTS? Consequently the sermon theme announced for that morning is: "WE NEED INNER STABILITY." It will be another of the series of sermons announced some weeks ago that deal with a real, practical application of our Christian gospel to the needs of this present day. And while we're on the subject of morning sermons, may I remind you that February 22 is LAYMAN'S SUNDAY throughout the Church and the sermon will be about "LARGE LESSONS FROM A LITTLE LAYMAN"?

We're having wonderful crowds at First Church. You are missing truly inspiring services if you have not been there. Why not join this crowd of enthusiastic worshipers this week? I hope to greet you on this Anniversary Sunday. It will be a profitable day for all of us.

Faithfully thine,

Raymond Grant

Used by A. Raymond Grant, pastor First Methodist Church, Sacramento, Calif.

Such skill comes only from unremitting concern, untiring attentiveness, unrelenting devotion and perpetual practice.

Central Methodist Church--your Church!--loves you, is deeply concerned with your welfare, remembers you constantly in her prayers, and would fain respond to your every casual or urgent call, your slightest or most grievous need. Our ears are tuned to the sound of your spirit's struggle.

But Central Church is calling you, too. Whatever the distractions, however intense and clamorous the appeals to be less than your best, we trust you to hear the constant challenge of your Church and all that it represents--supremely the high call of your Christ.

Practice selective hearing! Listen to the call of your best! Hearken to your highest ideals! It's "Central Calling!"

Cordially yours,[45]

Dear Friend:

What does a man work for?

A pay envelope, the future, family, security, independence, the satisfaction of accomplishment? You have your own answer, just like the next fellow--and yet it is incomplete, unsatisfying . . .

Far and above the desires of our workaday world, we are striving for something. It eludes definition. It has never been pictured on a chart. No microscope has revealed it. Rather, it is a deep longing to climb to a higher plane of living, to tune ourselves with eternal values.

Some folks feel a need for something better, yet they often go to the wrong sources for meeting that need. There are people who hope to find the answer in thrills--but those have a

[45] Henry Hitt Crane, pastor Central Methodist Church, Detroit, Mich.

way of becoming flat and uninteresting. Others believe that by increasing their possessions they have the answer--but they are often miserable. And then some people hope that by increasing their power and prestige that they will solve this mysterious longing. And yet, "uneasy lies the head that wears a crown."

Many years ago the early Christians sang these words as the morning hymn in their services: "O God, thou art my God; early will I seek thee: my soul thirsteth for thee, my flesh longeth for thee in a dry and thirsty land."

"My soul thirsteth for thee." Isn't that what we say deep in our lives? There is nothing else that can satisfy. God is the true portion of the soul. How he gives us peace and contentment --a "peace . . . which passeth all understanding."

You see, religion isn't just a creed, just a belief. We must realize that it is a transforming access of power. As Paul said, "I can do all things through Christ which strengtheneth me."

Here, then, is the secret of life and the title to glory. It is very simple, but all-sufficient. Let us press steadily onward, day by day "looking to Jesus." And thus by faith in Christ we not only overcome the world but we inherit heaven. Let us choose him and make his life our daily pattern. May we fill our hearts with a great love for Christ! Finally, let us sense the eternal significance in our daily work and in our opportunities of service to him and to all mankind.

That's what we are all working for.

Sincerely yours,

Postscripts Worth Pondering

D O YOU like to see your name misspelled? No, of course not, and neither does the other person. When in doubt about the way to address a person, try to follow his preferences. The fact that "M. H. Endicott" signs his name in this form is sufficient proof that it is his preference. He may not like to be addressed as "M. Harvey Endicott," and he may become irritated when addressed as "Malcolm Harvey Endicott." When you know only the surname of an individual to whom you wish to write, make every attempt possible to ascertain the given name or initials.

~

Although not recommended for general use, novel salutations are desirable for some types of letters. Sales promotion and advertising writers believe that unique beginnings are better attention-getters than conventional ones. For example: "Good Morning, Mrs. Anderson," "Greetings, Mrs. Anderson," or "A penny for your thoughts, Mrs. Anderson." In some form letters you will use salutations such as "Dear Member," "Dear Friend," or "Dear Member of First Church." Obviously they are impersonal, but they are adaptable for large mailings.

~

The first requirement for any successful church letter is enough attention value and interest to keep it out of the wastebasket until it has been read. "Attention value begins with the envelope, not the letter," William H. Butterfield, nationally known authority on letters, reminds us. To give an envelope "eye appeal," he suggests: (1) Use an individually typewritten address. (2) When possible, send your letter first class. (3) Use high-quality stationery in important mailings. Each envelope should always carry the sender's return address.

~

Who signs your letters? The signature exerts a definite influence on the reader—either positive or negative. If a letter is worth anything, it should have a written signature at the bottom. Even a mimeographed message is strengthened with a written signature. That of the pastor, chairman of the board, head of the Loyalty Sunday committee, or someone else in a position of authority and importance makes a strongly favorable impression on the average reader. See that the name is typed at the bottom of the letter, with the written signature above it. You may be proud of your signature and imagine that everyone can identify it, but to some stranger it may resemble the trade name of a Chinese breakfast food.

~

It is proverbial that first impressions count. Ask your printer (you can tell if he is competent by asking him to show you samples) to design an attractive letterhead for you. See that it is simple and in good taste. If possible, use a small cut of your church. An overcrowded heading makes the letter look heavy and unattractive. Avoid a gaudy display of type and illustration. It may cost you a little more to have a good-looking, dignified letterhead, but it will be worth its cost and more in creating favorable impressions.

~

No matter how well a letter is prepared, an unsatisfactory mailing list is a serious handicap in any mail program. Constant attention must be given to a list if it is to be kept up-to-date and reasonably efficient. Have you checked your mailing list recently? If not, there is an immense amount of lost motion in your program. Every list you use should be checked at least twice a year, more frequently if possible. In checking your list be sure to verify the given name or initials of each person. See that no "waste" is present by removing duplications, names of persons who have died, and names of those who transferred their membership or for other reasons are no longer actively associated with the church. Check off the returns of undelivered letters. See that changes reported to the church office are made immediately. Keep your mailing lists accurate and up-to-date, and your letter program will show more satisfactory results.

~

Now that you've read so far in this book you are probably saying, "Yes, I know that individually typed, personalized letters are best, but I must rely for the most part on form letters in my church program." Well, don't worry, because you can use form letters to advantage. You can give each kind of form letter a personalized element through its tone and attitude—by writing in a courteous and friendly manner. This can be done in mimeographed, printed, or multigraphed letters. To make the most of a form letter, give it just as many advantages of an individually typed letter as possible. Sign each letter personally, use first-class mail, use a high quality of paper, and see that each sheet is free from physical defects. If your list for this particular mailing is small, you can give each letter added strength by typing in the inside address and the salutation. Many a good writer has used the form letter to achieve the impossible. So can you!

~

Plutarch would have probably been an excellent letter writer. On one occasion he said: "To sing the same tune, as the saying is, is in everything cloying and offensive; but men are generally pleased with variety." If we are mentally lazy, we are likely to get into the habit of carelessly using words and phrases that will fit almost any situation. We know the danger of using rubber-stamp talk in letters. Usually the trouble is not with the word or phrase, it is that we habitually overwork it. So drop your mossy, overworked expressions. Give your personality a chance to shine through. Then you'll be singing a different tune.

~

No minister would think of emphasizing ten main points in a sermon, yet he may send out a letter with a handful of enclosures. When a reader receives such a mass of material, he may look at one for an instant, read part of the letter, then glance at another enclosure, and by that time is probably dazed by the whole thing. Too many extra pieces detract from the purpose of the letter. Direct-mail experts caution against the use of more than two or three enclosures in each letter. Whatever type of enclosure is used, be certain that it brings out some interesting point or points of your proposal as told in your letter. It is a supplementary piece —it isn't mailed just for the ride.

～

What is the best time for mailing? To determine the answer to this question, you must consider the objective of the letter, to whom it is being sent, whether an immediate response is desired, and other factors. During the Christmas season, for instance, most mail deliveries are delayed because of the immense volume sent at that time of year. If possible, letters should be sent so that they will not reach any recipients on Monday, because that's the day most persons start their "grand rush" for another week. In most instances, mail your letters so that they will reach the recipients from Tuesday to Friday. Avoid large mailings to your entire membership during the summer vacation period and at other times when many of your people are out of the city.

～

Use of personal pronouns is a puzzling problem to some letter writers. Since they have been told to avoid the overuse of "I," many feel that they should substitute "we." You *must* use "I" in many letters. You can hardly write, "We talked with you on the telephone Friday night." But of course you can use the pronoun "we" when it refers to more than one individual, or to all those individuals who make up your church. Mark Twain once said: "Nobody is entitled to refer to himself as 'we' except kings, editors, and persons with tapeworms." It is ridiculous to use "the writer" or "the undersigned" for "I" or "me." So you will never say, "The writer will be in his study Tuesday afternoon and will be glad to see you." Sybil Lee Gilmore, quoted in the *Dartnell Bulletin,* stated: "One of the most glaring errors in business letters is the attempt to make a letter impersonal by avoiding personal pronouns. Of course, one should guard against too much repetition of the vertical pronoun—but business letters should sound personal and friendly." That's an excellent maxim for all who write church letters.

~

You will improve your letter program by consulting reference books which will answer many of the questions that arise. You probably have a dictionary in your study, but in addition you should have a good grammar, a secretarial handbook, and a copy of *Roget's Thesaurus.* Regular use of these books will remove much of the guesswork from your letter writing.

~

Often you can get additional attention value by adding some novel touch to your letter. On some mailings you can staple, clip, or paste a short note or memo at the top of the letter. This is known as "flagging" a letter. Occasionally you may write a brief, yet personal, "P. S." at the bottom of a number of letters. One pastor clips miniature photographs of his church to certain mailings. Whatever method you use, be certain that it has a definite tie-in with your letter.

~

What is the chief fault of run-of-the-mill mimeographed letters? That's easy. Most of them are illegible in spots. With a little more care they could have been clear-cut, and thus would have made a much better impression. The best written letter is handicapped when it is smudged and foggy. But even an average letter has increased readability when it is neat and has sharp impressions.

~

There's nothing like a little competition to gain the co-operation of your associates and members. For the sake of variety, why not award prizes for the three best letters written for your next financial campaign? In all probability you have several good letter writers in your congregation. Find out who they are, encourage them, and put them to work. Follow this suggestion and your letters—even though they contain certain ideas which are used again and again —will have a fresh approach.

~

By all means, keep a file of letters of all types. Keep samples of your most effective letters, and also those used by other churches. When you have collected quite a few letters, it may be wise to classify them under general subjects, such as (1) loyalty, (2) stewardship, (3) collection, (4) congratulation, (5) special seasons, (6) special appeals, (7) adjustment, (8) good will. As you read magazines and other publications, check material which may be used in letters. Soon your file will grow, and before you know it you will have letters and ideas for all occasions.

Suggested Reference Material

Buck, Charles E. *The Business Letter-Writer's Manual*. New York: Doubleday, Doran & Co., 1938.

Buckley, Earle A. *How to Sell by Mail*. New York: McGraw-Hill Book Co., 1938.

Buckley, Homer J., and others. *Effective "Y" Letters*. New York: Association Press, 1943.

Butterfield, William H. *Effective Personal Letters*. New York: Prentice-Hall, Inc., 1945.

————. *12 Ways to Write Better Letters*. Norman: University of Oklahoma Press, 1943.

Crippen, John K. *Successful Direct-Mail Methods*. New York: McGraw-Hill Book Co., 1936.

Frailey, Lester E. *Smooth Sailing Letters*. New York: Prentice-Hall, 1938.

Harral, Stewart. *Public Relations for Churches*. New York and Nashville: Abingdon-Cokesbury Press, 1945.

Hutchinson, Lois I. *Standard Handbook for Secretaries*. New York: McGraw-Hill Book Co., 1936.

Parkhurst, C. C., and Blais, A. A. *English for Business*. New York: Prentice-Hall, 1944.

Smart, W. K., and McKelvey, L. W. *Business Letters*. New York: Harper & Bros., 1941.

Swartz, Marcel M. *How to Write Successful Business Letters*. New York: Franklin Watts, 1944.

Taintor, S. A., and Monro, K. M. *The Secretary's Handbook*. New York: The Macmillan Co., 1938.

Index